PENGUIN BOOKS

THIRTY SECONDS

Michael J. Arlen is the author of *Living-Room War* (1969; described by *The New York Times* as "the only good book ever written about television"); *Exiles* (1970; nominated for a National Book Award); *An American Verdict* (1973); *Passage to Ararat* (1975; winner of a National Book Award for contemporary affairs); and *The View from Highway 1* (1976). Mr. Arlen has been television critic for *The New Yorker* since 1966.

Michael J. Arlen

THIRTY
SECONDS

PENGUIN BOOKS

Penguin Books Ltd, Harmondsworth,
Middlesex, England
Penguin Books, 40 West 23rd Street,
New York, New York 10010, U.S.A.
Penguin Books Australia Ltd, Ringwood,
Victoria, Australia
Penguin Books Canada Limited, 2801 John Street,
Markham, Ontario, Canada L3R 1B4
Penguin Books (N.Z.) Ltd, 182–190 Wairau Road,
Auckland 10, New Zealand

First published in the United States of America by
Farrar, Straus & Giroux 1980
First published in Canada by
McGraw-Hill Ryerson Limited 1980
Published in Penguin Books 1981
Reprinted 1982, 1984

LIBRARY OF CONGRESS CATALOGING IN PUBLICATION DATA
Arlen, Michael J
   Thirty seconds.
   Reprint of the 1980 ed. published by Farrar, Straus & Giroux,
New York.
   1. Advertising agencies—United States—Case studies.   I. Title.
[HF6182.U5A74   1980]   659.1′125′0973   80-25226
ISBN 0 14 00.5810 9

Printed in the United States of America by
Offset Paperback Mfrs., Inc., Dallas, Pennsylvania
Set in Baskerville

The text of this book originally appeared in *The New Yorker*.

To Sara Spencer

THIRTY
SECONDS

You Can Do Whatever You Want

T HERE IS PROBABLY SOMETHING TO BE SAID FOR
starting this story near its real beginning—say, with
Mr. C. E. Lilly at the Lilly Welding Shop in Ozona,
Texas, back in 1966. But for practical purposes (and
this is nothing if not a story of practicality, one way or
another) we may as well start a little closer to the
present day—in the spring of 1979, outside an old dark-
green double-width door to what was surely once a
coach house or garage, on a quiet, dilapidated side
street in New York's East Fifties, close by the river.

Let us open the door. Inside, in near-darkness, are
another door, set in a brick wall, and, beside that door,
an open entranceway to a steep, narrow flight of stairs
leading down.

We descend the stairs into a brightly lit room—no,
into a series of rooms; in fact, an office, with fluorescent tubes gleaming in its ceiling. Young women, almost all of them talking on telephones, sit at or stand

beside white Formica desks. Men, also mostly young, and mostly attired in bluejeans, work shirts, and sneakers, move through the office, in between the white Formica desks, some of them carrying clipboards, or Styrofoam cups of coffee, or metal cases of camera equipment, or sometimes nothing at all. We pass through this office area, with its bright—indeed, overbright—lighting, its whiteness, its air of cheerful modernity, and go down a little corridor to an old-fashioned dark wood door. This leads, as we open it, into a middle-sized room, comparatively dim (no fluorescent lights), which has an even more old-fashioned air about it—its walls being covered with Maxfield Parrish prints and an array of what seem to be nineteenth-century school photographs—and which contains, seated around a large oak table that is laden with bowls of fresh fruit, a platter of cheese, and bottles of Perrier, about a dozen men and women.

This is the conference room of Steve Horn, Inc., whose brightly lit offices are outside, and whose studios (mostly filled with props and camera equipment) are on the floor above, inside the green garage door. Steve Horn himself is seated at the head of the table, with half a glass of Perrier in front of him. Even seated, he seems to be a big man, with a large, heavy-boned face (somewhat reminiscent of the late character actor Ward Bond), with a thick brown mustache that stops just short of a handlebar, and with a similarly thick brown head of hair, brushed straight back; his appearance is subtly Western—an effect that is possibly unintended, though not diminished by a gray neckerchief he wears above a work shirt, and boots that stick out from beneath olive-green work pants.

Next to Horn on his left—as at a dinner party, which the conference vaguely resembles, because of the food and drink in the center of the table—sits his wife and partner, a pretty, dark-haired, solemn-eyed woman in her late thirties named Linda. Beyond Linda, in clockwise order, sit the following people: Ray, Joan, Cheryl, Michael, and Alayne, who all work for Steve Horn, and Gaston, Jerry, and Elliott, who all work for the N. W. Ayer advertising agency. Two of the agency people, Gaston and Jerry, wear bluejeans and open-necked sports shirts, but with regular shoes instead of sneakers or boots. The third agency man, Elliott, wears what might be called traditional city clothes, but without a jacket, for he has hung his jacket on the back of his chair; he is the only man in the room who looks as if he were actually in business in New York.

The purpose of the meeting is to discuss locations for a series of five television commercials, each thirty seconds long, that Steve Horn, who is a director of filmed television commercials, will be shooting for N. W. Ayer and its client, American Telephone & Telegraph.

Alayne is speaking (she is a woman in her early thirties, with tortoiseshell eyeglasses and a broad, open Irish face) : "Look, the Long Island Game Farm is fantastic, but the problem is we can't use the camel."

Gaston says: "O.K., we cancel the camel."

Linda says: "How about llamas?"

Steve says: "Llamas are terrific. I like llamas, except they spit."

Jerry says: "How badly do we need llamas?"

Alayne says: "Actually, research says kids only remember the little things they can pick up—the cuddly bunnies. Research says if you show a little kid a llama or a camel he usually doesn't remember he's seen one."

Jerry says: "What does he think he's seen?"

Gaston says: "I think a mix might do something for us. How about if we had a kangaroo in the background?"

Steve says: "I don't see that we need a kangaroo."

Alayne says: "Anyway, they don't have a kangaroo."

Gaston says: "O.K., cancel the kangaroo."

A maid brings in a tray of little cookies and some cans of Coke and Dr Pepper. Ray and Michael take Cokes. Jerry, Gaston, and Steve take some of the little cookies.

Steve says: "Let's see, where do we stand on the zoo?"

Linda says: "Vincent is Polaroiding it this afternoon."

Steve says: "O.K. I think now we ought to talk grandmothers. I think we've got some problem with grandmothers."

Gaston says: "I don't see that we have any big problem."

Steve says: "Well, we've got film on every available grandmother in the country right here in the office."

Linda says: "The trouble is each grandmother has been used so many times."

Steve says: "So it seems to me we have three or four grandmothers that are interchangeable—except, of course, for the black grandmother. I think the grandmother-and-grandfather situation needs to be worked out carefully. I also need to know how much time I have for the dissolves."

Jerry says: "You can do whatever you want."

Steve says: "Do we have twelve seconds?"

Gaston says: "I think you have eleven."

Steve says: "I could do it in seven."

Gaston says: "But if you develop an idea it's going to take at least eleven."

Linda says: "He can do it in eight."

Steve says: "Easy in eight. Seven would be pushing it."

Jerry says: "You have eleven. You can do whatever you want."

Now a couple of problems come up with one of the thirty-second commercials which has been provisionally titled "Tap Dancing."

"Tap Dancing" is a so-called vignette commercial, as are many television commercials these days. This means that instead of presenting a generally coherent narrative (as, for example, the Löwenbräu-beer commercials do) it consists of a sequence of only slightly interlocking little scenes and situations: in this case, five situations and ten scenes—of which one scene, according to the script prepared by the N. W. Ayer agency, has a young Army recruit talking on the phone in his barracks.

Steve says: "I'm worried about that telephone. You mean he has it by his bedside?"

Jerry says: "Well, there could be a phone in the entry hall."

Alayne says: "Ray was down researching Fort Dix and McGuire Air Force Base, and the problem is, in the new barracks they only have phones outside, and in the old barracks they don't have phones anywhere except in the PX."

Gaston says: "Why don't we do the PX? That might make a kind of nice effect."

Alayne says: "The problem is, all the PXs have changed. They're all new, and they're all big concrete things that look like Alexander's."

Elliott says: "You mean, guys don't go anywhere to get hamburgers anymore?"

Alayne says: "I guess they go to the new PXs."

Gaston says: "Sure. They'd always have to have a place to sell hamburgers. They probably have a hamburger place in there somewhere."

Elliott says: "A cafeteria—a cafeteria is what they'd have."

Steve says: "Look, I thought we were talking about telephones. How about using West Point? That might be a nice touch—all that tradition."

Linda says: "I don't think the cadets at West Point have telephones by their beds, either."

Steve says: "Do you actually know that? O.K., how

about instead of an Army guy we have him a rich kid at military school?"

Alayne says: "The problem is, military schools are on the way out."

Jerry says: "Maybe we could still do something with West Point or Annapolis. After all, the phone doesn't have to be just by the guy's bed."

Steve says: "It might be better *not* by his bed. I mean, would it look military with the guy lounging in the sack?"

Gaston says: "Nobody ever said he was *in* the bed."

Steve says: "O.K., Alayne, check out West Point—I don't see we need Annapolis. Check and see if they have entry phones. We could have sort of a cute scene, don't you think? All that tradition."

The Casual, Positive Aspect

J ERRY'S LAST NAME IS PFIFFNER, WHICH IS PRO-
nounced more easily than it reads: thus—"fifner." He
is about six feet tall, with a modest fringe of beard,
and is generally quiet-spoken and almost professorial
in his demeanor, though there is a stolidity and mat-
ter-of-factness to his opinions and general point of
view which doubtless derive from his upbringing—in
Iowa, where he was born and raised and went to college. He is forty-five years old and is at present a fairly
important figure at N. W. Ayer. A senior vice-president on the creative side of the agency, he is the leader
of a Creative Group (Gaston and Elliott and thirteen
others) whose responsibility it has been to devise the
advertising for A.T.&T.'s new campaign.

Jerry Pfiffner is seated at his desk in the N. W. Ayer
offices, which extend over seven floors of Burlington
House, on Sixth Avenue at Fifty-fourth Street, close by
the three network buildings and also the Time-Life

Building—an area that is clearly the new "Madison Avenue" of New York. His office is not especially large or imposing; there is no antechamber, no watchdog secretary to defend the door. It is a typical executive office, one might say, in a company that doubtless has an abundance of executives: it contains a large oak table, beige carpeting, several modern-style chairs, and four grade-school children's drawings affixed with tape to a side wall.

"Basically, I'm a new man on the A.T.&T. account," Jerry says. "By that I mean that it's been in the agency for decades but I've only been working on it for the past year. Before that, I worked mostly in packaged goods—for example, campaigns for Kraft foods or various Nestlé products. The last campaign I directed was Sunrise Coffee, for Nestlé. This was a new product—a new kind of instant coffee, containing chicory. So our basic challenge was to develop a creative strategy that would appeal to chicory users as well as non-users. Right away, we decided on *non-bitter*. Right away, before even getting into the chicory thing, we figured we at least had to promise people *non-bitter* coffee. Then we went to our research people to find out about chicory, and what they told us was that almost nobody had ever heard of chicory. I mean, it wasn't being used for this, it wasn't being used for that; in fact, almost nobody seemed to know anything about it from a user point of view. So research said we could say pretty much what we wanted to about it. For a while, we thought about saying *smoothness*, but the fact is we didn't really know why chicory made coffee smoother, or even if it did. So we asked ourselves, 'What else besides non-bitter can we say about the coffee?,' and somebody said, '*Non-phony*'—meaning it wasn't a phony, it was natural. Well, we didn't want to say *natural*, since everything else in the stores was 'natural,' so we decided on *better-natured*." Jerry gets up from his desk and reaches over to a shelf on the wall behind him for a jar with a red-and-yellow label, which he sets in the center of the desk. It is a jar of Sunrise Coffee, bearing the slogan "Better Natured Not Bitter."

"There's a lot of challenge in packaged goods," says Jerry, sitting down again, "but it's a special, direct kind of challenge. New products come on-stream all the time and also go down the drain all the time, so your principal thrust is how to *position* the product— how to figure out what's unique about the new coffee or the new yogurt, and then how to put a name on it and package it. I was happy to move over to the Long Lines account—that's what A.T.&T. calls its long-distance operations—because I wanted a change of direction, something with greater emotional texture. Right away, with Long Lines, you start thinking in terms of feelings and emotions. From the very beginning, A.T.&T. wanted us to overcome the negative emotions associated with long-distance—you know, the way people used to think about the high cost of long-distance, the bad-news phone call in the middle of the night. For years, there has been a definitely *negative, uncasual* quality to a lot of long-distance calling. A.T.&T. wanted us to emphasize the *casual, positive* aspect: long-distance is fun, it's easy, it's cheap. Of course, we didn't want to be sentimental, we wanted to be upbeat and to get across an image kind of thing: people calling for fun; people calling for no reason at all—not just family talking to family but friends talking to friends. So, strategy-wise, we started with a kind of two-faced objective: the casual thing and the people-calling-outside-the-family thing. And right up front we were thinking also maybe a musical thing. There was a lot of up-front input about music; even the marketing guys were thinking it should be primarily a musical approach—maybe with something like the McDonald's theme, only different. In the agency, we started work over a year ago, back around January 1978: at first, not so much nuts-and-bolts work as thinking and theorizing—trying to figure out, what were we really trying to say, what were the basic emotions, and how could we keep them keyed to strategy? We used a lot of writers and a lot of art directors. We tried hundreds of approaches. We tried approaches that were musical and nonmusical, that were humorous and nonhumorous. We tried celebrities and noncelebrities. We had I don't know how many meetings; it seemed as if for months we were always having meetings. And all this time we were looking for the right theme line. By April 7, 1978, we'd narrowed the field down to four theme lines. Speaking personally, I thought the choice all along was between just two of them: the 'Reach Out' theme we ended up using and 'Keep in Touch, America.' So, late in April, we went out to the client and presented our final selections and frankly admitted that we were split ourselves—we were a house divided. In my opinion, any one of our four finalists could have worked just as well. In the end, as I suspected, it came down to a horse race between 'Reach Out' and 'Keep in Touch,' and the final vote went to 'Reach Out,' because the consensus seemed to be that if there was one thing that America didn't need at that time it was more America-oriented advertising. I'm happy with the 'Reach Out' theme, because it's simple, with emotional content, and it emphasizes the human factor: it speaks to people. I guess you could say I came up with the basic line, though when you work in a group you get a lot of input from everyone else. The thing about writing theme lines is that, creatively speaking, they almost never just happen when you sit down at the typewriter—not like body copy. Sometimes, though, they come up and surprise you, and that's where the magic is."

The One-Hundred-and-Ninety-fourth Time

J UST ABOUT EVERY DIRECTOR OF COMMERCIALS HAS HIS
Reel. (One should probably say "his or her" Reel, but
there is no evidence—at least in the standard "yellow
book" listing of directors of commercials—of there being any females in that branch of the profession.) A
Reel is a particular reel of film: an anthology of the
director's best work (in his opinion), which serves the
function of an artist's portfolio, or a salesman's sample
case, when he is looking for business. In different cir-
cumstances, when, in April 1979—roughly a year after
client approval was given to the basic "Reach Out"
theme—further client approval had been given to the
"Tap Dancing" commercial, Jerry Pfiffner might well
have called in Gaston Braun, the member of his Creative Group who functions as senior producer, and
asked him to find a director for the commercial, and
Braun might then have phoned a number of production companies (there are roughly four hundred of

them in New York, according to the "yellow book")
and asked the directors to send over their Reels, so
that the agency could decide which one of them should
handle the filming. In fact, Jerry did ask Gaston to find
a director for the new project, and Gaston got in touch
with three of the top men in the business—Steve Horn,
Bob Giraldi, and Rick Levine—before finally settling
on Steve Horn. But there was never any question of
asking for Reels from veterans of such stature. "These
guys are right up there at the peak of the profession,"
says Gaston. "We know their work. We could have
gone with any one of them, but for this particular job
we were hoping for Steve, because he's so good with
the emotional things." Horn was scheduled to finish a
Coke shoot early in May and was due to start on a
Burger King shoot on a later date in May, so he figured
he could do the A.T.&T. filming in between. It was all
settled on the phone. After all, would you ask Michael
Cimino to submit a sample of his work before signing
him to a new project? (Actually, if you did, you might
hope, though perhaps in vain, to see some of the commercials for Pepsi-Cola and United Airlines which
Cimino filmed when he was a director of commercials
in New York.)

For the record, however, and maybe because he is
mindful that what goes up in the advertising business
sometimes also comes down, Steve Horn still has his
Reel; in fact, he has several Reels, which include the
following commercials:

(1) A commercial for Coca-Cola in which a number of people, mostly young, are sitting or standing (and singing) on the windowsills of an old brick apartment building.

(2) A commercial for Schaefer beer in which the hockey player Bobby Hull skates the length of an empty rink (under the center of which is an enormous Schaefer emblem) and fires a shot past the goalie.

(3) A stark, hardboiled commercial for the Mayor's Narcotics Control Council, filmed in black and white, showing some young people (presumably not those in the Coke ad) shooting up in a back alley.

(4) A commercial for Johnson & Johnson about a baby and baby oil.

(5) A commercial for Volvo cars, humorous in tone, in which a little Volvo departs from a great house in the country (butler and maids in the background) , only to meet—and, of course, survive—the hazards of rainstorms and road dangers in the world outside.

(6) A commercial for Mutual of New York in which a youthful John Travolta is sweeping up in an empty luncheonette while a somber voice intones, "He was going to do the studying while you'd do the saving. He didn't count on your dying quite so soon." (This was Travolta's last commercial—at least, as an unknown actor—and there is some feeling of pride in Steve Horn's office that it doubtless helped to put him on the path to media stardom.)

(7) Two strenuously artistic commercials for the Metropolitan Life Insurance Company, each set near the turn of the century, each with a nostalgic, gauzy look to it, and each having to do with nursing care and disease prevention.

(8) A humorous commercial for Tonka Toys.

(9) A stylish commercial for Great Western Champagne.

(10) A commercial for Miller beer showing a brightly blazing building on a waterfront, with firemen from a fireboat putting out the fire and then heading into a cheery, masculine bar to have a round of Miller beer.

Steve Horn on the subject of beer commercials: "I like doing beer ads; they have a good feel to them—don't ask me why. I've done Miller, Löwenbräu, Schaefer. Sure, Miller and Schaefer are competitors. I also do 7Up and Coke. Everybody does competitors. I guess on the outside some of the agencies and clients get very uptight and competitive—you know, Macy's won't talk to Gimbel's—but on the inside, where the stuff is put together, I guess everybody deals, like everywhere else. The only problem I ever have is with the props. I mean, the waterfront-fire thing was hard. You don't find an old building that you can film a fire in so easily. And you need to borrow a fireboat and some Fire Department guys to supervise the fire. Then, the Bobby Hull ad for Schaefer was hard. Not Bobby Hull. He's a peach. Very helpful. Always trying. But that damn Schaefer logo we had under the ice—

Well, we were up shooting in the New Haven Coliseum and we had these canvas things under the ice. I mean, the logo came in sections, and the ice wasn't freezing right, and then every time Bobby skated over it some part of the logo would sort of come unstuck. I don't think we ever really did get it just right. I mean, if you look closely you can see the logo sort of drift apart as Bobby comes over it. Speaking of hard, there was one ad we did for Miller Lite that just about bust me. It was about a pool player, I think his name was Steve Mizerak. I don't know where they got him, I guess he's a real pro, but that day he just couldn't do anything right. I mean, he had this one shot to do, a pretty tricky shot—I sure couldn't do it, but I'm not supposed to be a pool player—where he bounces the cue ball off a couple of other balls and a couple of cushions and then it travels back across the table toward a corner pocket, where there's a bottle of Miller Lite in front of the pocket, and then, just before the cue ball hits the bottle, Mizerak lifts the bottle and the ball is supposed to pop into the pocket. All the while, mind you, Mizerak is speaking his lines. 'A lot of people don't think pool is strenuous,' he says, lining up his fancy shot, 'but you can work up a real good sweat,' he says, sending the ball off on its run, 'even when you're just showin' off,' he says, holding the bottle as the ball drops into the pocket. Well, I'm telling you, he tried that shot one hundred and ninety-three times and it didn't work once. I know it was one hundred and ninety-three times, because I was counting.

We set up at seven o'clock in the morning and we were still there at seven that evening. I mean, that ball went everywhere except where it was supposed to. Wrong pockets. Wrong direction. Off the table. Mizerak was dying. We were dying. Then, the one-hundred-and-ninety-fourth time, he got it. Boy, you should have heard the applause from the other actors! I mean, they were supposed to applaud a little, but this time they really let go—such *relief*. I said, 'That's it. We go home.' It made a nice ad, too—a lot of feeling. Maybe all that tension added something, I don't know. It sure as hell was a long day for a glass of beer.''

Can You Do a Yoga Headstand?

IT IS THREE O'CLOCK ON A WARM MAY AFTERNOON, and the three Ayer creative people—Jerry Pfiffner, Gaston Braun, and Elliott Manketo—together with an assistant named Eddie, are seated inside a small, narrow, dark, windowless, and generally uncomfortable room looking at a little television screen. The room is officially known as the Control Room—in fact, it is one of five studios in the Ayer offices—though its appearance is more that of a storeroom for sundry unused items of electronic equipment. For instance, on a shelf near Gaston are three television-playback machines, two medium-sized television sets, two tape machines, and numerous cassettes. Toward the back of the room is a litter of sound-recording equipment. Behind that is a movie projector, and strips of film hang from an overhead wire. Jerry, Gaston, and Elliott are seated side by side near the front of the narrow room on steel-frame cafeteria-style chairs, with Gaston holding a clipboard on his lap and Jerry a half-eaten sandwich and Elliott a can of Diet Pepsi. Behind them, Eddie sits at a table, with another television-playback machine before him: obedient to Eddie's touch, the spool of tape in the machine unwinds and rewinds, feeding directly to the little TV screen that the three men are watching.

What is taking place is part of the casting process for "Tap Dancing." The over-all procedure began about a week before, soon after the meeting in Steve Horn's conference room. Mind you, not only is Steve Horn the director and chief cameraman but his office, Steve Horn, Inc., is the production company: a free-lance enterprise that the N. W. Ayer agency has hired to see to it that the script for "Tap Dancing" gets turned into film. Horn's office, accordingly, handles nearly all the production-related details, such as locations, wardrobe, props, and casting, though a kind of governing approval rests with the agency and, of course, final approval rests with the client. Thus, what has happened is this: Michael Pepino, the member of Horn's staff who handles casting, first checked the script for principal-actor parts (for instance, a barber; a cowboy; two girls, one black, one white, to do a yoga scene) and then phoned the dozen or so better-known talent agencies and outlined his basic requirements. The talent agencies then called the people on their lists who fitted the general categories—mainly of age and sex, it would seem—and soon afterward a stream of actors and would-be actors came down the stairs to Steve Horn,

Inc., where the aspirants sat on two stylish, not hugely comfortable wooden benches waiting their turn to be asked to step into a room at the foot of the stairs which contained a faded green couch, a chair, and a videotape camera. One by one, the auditioning actors did their stuff for the videotape camera (operated by Michael), the resulting spools of videotaped auditions to be checked through later, first by Steve Horn and then by the agency.

Right now, on the little TV screen in the Ayer studio, Jerry, Gaston, and Elliott are looking over auditions of white girls for the yoga scene.

"O.K., who's next?" says Jerry.

Gaston checks his clipboard. "One-eighty-three," he says. "Tatiana King."

"Tatiana?" says Elliott.

"That's what it says," says Gaston.

Eddie punches the tape machine forward, and a black-and-white picture of a young woman in a skirt and blouse appears on the screen. The woman is standing, her arms at her sides, against a bare wall, with just a hint of an old couch in the background.

Offscreen, a man's voice, presumably Michael's, says, "What's your name?"

"Tatiana King," says the girl, flashing a big, wide smile.

"Agency?"

"J. Michael Bloom."

"Can you do a yoga headstand?"

"I sure can," says the girl, flashing another smile.

"O.K., now," says the offscreen voice. "First I want smiles and happy. Then I want a bit sad but not *too* sad. Then I want real happy."

"Like she's an old roommate?" says the girl.

"Sure," says the voice. "Now pick up the phone."

The girl reaches out of camera range for the receiver of a telephone, and brings it close to the side of her head. "Do you want me to tuck it in?" she says.

"It doesn't matter," says the voice. "Whatever's comfortable."

"It's comfortable like this," says the girl.

"You can start now," says the voice. "Ring-ring."

The girl flashes another big, wide smile, for the camera, and launches into what is clearly improvised dialogue: "Oh, hi. *Hi!* It's so *good* to hear from you. I mean, it's *really good!* It's been ages, hasn't it? What have you been *doing?* . . . Oh, you have a *job?*"

"Now switch over to the sad," says the voice.

"You've had *troubles?*" says the girl, reversing the smile into a look of extreme dismay. "Oh, that's *terrible*. I mean, that's *really terrible*."

"Not too sad," says the voice.

"But I *bet* it's gonna work out," says the girl. "I'm *sure* it's gonna work out."

"Now real happy," says the voice.

"You're going to get *married!*" says the girl, flashing the big smile again and rocking her head back and forth with joyful laughter. "Oh, that's *so wonderful*. That's the best news I ever heard. That's *really won-*

derful. I can't *wait* to meet him. That's really *wonderful*."

"O.K.," says the voice.

The girl in the skirt and blouse disappears from the screen and is replaced by another girl, this one tall and lanky, and wearing jeans and a T-shirt.

"What's your name?" says the offscreen voice.

"Eliza Walsh," says the girl.

Gaston turns in his chair. "What did you think of Tatiana?" he says.

Eddie punches the tape machine to a stop.

"I'd say she was a standard," says Jerry.

"She reminded me of some Procter & Gamble girl," says Elliott. "Or like that girl we used on that shampoo thing."

"We've never used this one," says Gaston.

"Definitely too Procter & Gamble," says Jerry.

"Next one, Eddie," says Gaston.

The girl on the TV screen comes to life again. The instructions that were issued to Tatiana are repeated. This girl, too, puts the fake phone to her head. She, too, smiling and laughing, launches into an improvised patter: "Oh, I don't *believe* it. It's been so *long*. It's been *ages*. How are you doin'? . . . Really *great?* . . . Oh, that's *wonderful*. . . . Oh, you've had a *problem?*"

The girls come and go as the afternoon passes—though there is no sense of time passing in the little room, and also, strangely, no real sense of impatience on the part of the three observers, except for some periodic shifting and wriggling in the steel-frame chairs, and except that Jerry occasionally goes to the back of the room to make or receive a phone call.

One call is apparently from Steve Horn.

"We're looking at the yoga girls," says Jerry into the phone. "I think a couple are definitely maybes, but we haven't seen a real winner yet. . . . West Point doesn't check out? What do you mean? . . . They've got to have phones somewhere. . . . I see. What about Annapolis? . . . I see. O.K., well, let's keep trying. That sounds real noisy where you are. . . . I see. O.K., take care."

Jerry comes back to his chair. The tape machine has been stopped in mid-audition for the phone call.

"What about West Point?" says Gaston.

"The Army said it was O.K., provided we only shoot outside," says Jerry.

"But there aren't any phones outside," says Gaston.

"Right," says Jerry. "Who are we looking at?"

"Two-fifty-five," says Gaston, checking his clipboard. "Sidney Bowles."

"Have you noticed?" says Elliott. "The only Sidneys left in the world are all women."

"What about Annapolis?" says Gaston.

"Worse than West Point," says Jerry.

On the TV screen, Sidney Bowles is doing her bit with the phone. "Oh, yes, that's so *wonderful*, that's *so good* to hear, no, I really *mean* it, that's just *great*." Her smile, which is wide and frequent, seems somehow less strained than some of the others'; her looks, though, are not especially striking.

"Not a bad look," says Jerry.

"It's different," says Gaston. "I'll put 'maybe.' "

"She might even be a yes," says Jerry.

"A maybe," says Elliott. "Sidney Bowles is a natural maybe. Where was Steve calling from, anyway?"

"He's finished with that Coke shoot in Florida," says Jerry. "He said he was calling from a train."

"O.K., now," says Gaston. "I'd like us to get to two-eighty before we break. Eddie, let's go to two-fifty-six."

The new girl on the screen has long blond hair, which she keeps brushing away from her face. Her name is Mara Wells. When the offscreen voice asks her if she can do a yoga headstand, she replies, with a radiant smile, "You bet I can." Then asks, in a smaller, more practical voice, "Could you tell me just what is it you *mean* by a yoga headstand?"

Not Good Work for a Young Man

GASTON BRAUN IS FRENCH, AS HIS FIRST NAME indicates, but he left his native land some ten years ago, and has since become Americanized and thus more or less indistinguishable from his colleagues, save for a slight accent that unmistakably suggests his Gallic origins. Gaston is forty-one, with curly brownish hair; he is on the short side—not fat, or even stout, but definitely chunky, although with a certain bounce or springiness to his walk, which, combined with the faded bluejeans and short-sleeved navy-blue shirts he wears in warm weather as he goes about his business in the city, gives him a somewhat *sportif* appearance; nevertheless, an ever-present clipboard, or sometimes a bulging old leather briefcase, reveals him to be a man of affairs. He is a married man, as are his colleagues Jerry and Elliott, but, unlike them—they live in the suburbs—he lives on the West Side.

Gaston tells a little about himself: "I was born in

Nancy and grew up in Paris. The usual family life. The usual schooling. When I went to college, I wasn't really sure what I wanted to do afterward, so I studied political science. It seemed—how do you say?—relevant. Then, of course, I had to go into the French Army, and wandered around on maneuvers in the Black Forest—a dreadful place. After the Army—well, it seemed the only thing you could do with a political-science degree, at least in France, was either to learn more of it or to try to teach what you knew or to go to work for the government, none of which activities were very appealing at the time. So, while I was rather floundering about in Paris—not a bad period, really, but one of those youthful, drifting stages where you seem to be getting up later and later every morning—a fellow I knew who was getting ahead in one of the big French advertising agencies told me I should give advertising a try, because the agencies were looking for people with my kind of 'broad background' to be account executives. What he meant about my 'broad background' was that I could speak a couple of languages, including English. And he was right—those days, a 'broad background,' which chiefly meant being able to speak English, was what the Paris agencies were looking for. Now, of course, they don't care so much about it and want only business-school graduates. At any rate, I went to work for one of the big French agencies, and I became an account executive on the Procter & Gamble account—a junior account executive, I should say. It was a nice job in many ways, but Procter & Gamble in France is very like Procter & Gamble in America or Procter & Gamble anywhere else in the world; in other words, it's very regimented—in fact, it's very boring. Everything is controlled from the company headquarters, in Cincinnati. Periodically, they fly in all the senior account executives from agencies all over the world and give them the word. They call it a conference, but it's more like an indoctrination. But don't get me wrong—it was great training, great experience. I think if you can handle an account for Procter & Gamble you can do just about anything in this business. I was still a young man, though, and I got to the point where I couldn't take that kind of work anymore. It wasn't good work for a young man. So I quit account work and quit Procter & Gamble and switched to the creative side—to TV production. And when I came over here, in 1969, I stayed on the creative side. I've been with Ayer for the past nine years, all of it as a producer. I'm happy where I am. I don't think I'd ever want to go back to account work. Temperamentally, I'm very well adjusted to the creative side."

A Recording Session with

Phoebe Snow

A TEMPORARY DISTRACTION NOW OCCURS, IN THE form of a recording session with the pop-rock singer Phoebe Snow. This is for an A.T.&T. radio commercial—not TV—but the event has a special significance, partly because of the celebrity stature of Miss Snow, partly because the song to be recorded is the basic "Reach Out" theme itself. Miss Snow isn't the only popular singer who will be heard singing the A.T.&T. song, for the Ayer people have already recorded Roberta Flack and Ray Charles and in due course will record Jose Feliciano, Tammy Wynette, and Paul Williams; each of the six will be singing a different, individually styled arrangement of the "Reach Out" song, which started with Jerry Pfiffner's five-word theme line, "Reach out and touch someone," and was farmed out to the commercial song-writing team of Lucas-McFaul to be developed into a song, with music and lyrics—and later was further adapted into numerous variations for the television commercials. Thus, even though it is a relatively less expensive radio spot, the Phoebe Snow session has the look and feel of importance about it—the theme song is basic to the over-all media campaign—and so it draws as its audience (that is, in addition to Miss Snow and her retinue and the various people involved with the musical arrangements) not only Jerry Pfiffner but also Fred McClafferty and George Eversman, the senior Ayer men on the account side of the project, and there is a report that the client company itself will be represented: by Phil Shyposh, the advertising manager for A.T.&T. Long Lines.

The recording takes place in a studio in the West Fifties called Regent Sound Studios. This is one of those small, profitable, and largely invisible businesses that New York seems to abound in. Typically, there is an outer office of modest gentility, containing a secretary, a table with some magazines, and a couch; and then a door that leads into a quite different world of long, unprettified, unpainted, uncarpeted corridors with bare concrete walls, with occasional black doors, each marked "No Entrance," and with a scattered litter of soft-drink cans, and now and then a little pile of unused or discarded building tiles, or perhaps a roll of insulating fiber—the immediate effect being that of an East European city desultorily attempting minimal repairs after a long siege. But then, upon opening one of the doors marked "No Entrance"—or, in this instance, opening the right door—and entering, we are in yet another kind of world. Vanished is the frilly-bloused secretary, with her coffee cup and dusty rubber plant; forgotten are the drab, bombed-out East European corridors. We are now in a brightly lit room of no great size into which a dozen or more men and women have been tightly crammed, most of them standing around a large, beige, table-height electronic sound-mixing console, which occupies the center of the floor. Against a side wall is a bank of smaller machines and instruments, metallic gray for the most part, with little glass dials upon which needles are wagging back and forth. In the front of this room, which is the control room, is a huge panel or window of clear glass (indeed, this wall is mainly glass), through which one can look into a much larger room: clearly a recording studio, for it is filled with numerous pieces of musical equipment, such as a grand piano, an electronic piano, a synthesizer, and an assortment of drums; at least two dozen standing microphones and an assortment of music racks; and two people, a man and a woman, who are standing next to a separate microphone in the front of the studio, about ten feet from the glass panel. The man is Bill Eaton, a free-lance songwriter and arranger, who has worked out the special "Reach Out" arrangement for Miss Snow. The woman is Phoebe Snow herself: at first glance, a surprisingly mousy-looking young woman, perhaps in her late twenties, with frizzy brown hair, a pale face, big glasses, and a plumpish waist and behind, who is attired in bluejeans, a plain white shirt, and a brown vest, and is wearing headphones.

Inside the control room, an older man, rather natty in a plaid sports jacket and a black shirt, is speaking to Phoebe Snow through a little microphone on the mixing console. This is Elliot Lawrence, a composer and former bandleader, who now serves as chief musical consultant to the N. W. Ayer agency. "O.K., Phoebe," says Lawrence. "Let me know if the headphones are right."

Bill Eaton adjusts the headphones on Phoebe's frizzy hair. Phoebe waves her hand and makes a face to indicate that the headphones are fine.

"O.K., Bill," says Lawrence.

Bill Eaton waves, and leaves the studio.

"O.K., Phoebe," says Lawrence. "Let's do it."

Now, from speakers on the ceiling of the control room, and presumably also from the headphones on Phoebe Snow's head, comes a blast of sound: a loud, primitive bump-bump-bump that is repeated for a couple of measures, after which Phoebe starts singing, her voice coupled with the music:

> Reach out, reach out, and touch someone!
> Reach out, call up, and just say Hi!
> Reach out, reach out, and touch someone!
> Wherever you are,
> You're never too far.
> They're waiting to share your day.
> People from coast to coast,

34

> Calling up friends to keep them close.
> Families who care so much,
> Keeping in touch—
> Reach out, reach out, and touch someone!
> Reach out, reach out, and touch someone!

After the song is over, Phoebe shakes her head, apparently not happy with the way it went. The music is repeated, and she does it a second time. Then a third time. Then a fourth time. Then a fifth time.

Lawrence speaks to a man in a short-sleeved orange sports shirt who is sitting at the large sound-mixing console and operating its controls—pushing, pulling, adjusting dozens of little knobs and the like, in the manner of an organist or an airline pilot. This is Bob Liftin, the owner and president of Regent Sound Studios. "I think we'll leave it there for a moment," says Lawrence. "Let's hold that one and then let's make another." To Phoebe, he says through the microphone, "I think you were maybe a little serious that time. It sounded a little unhappy, just a shade too unhappy."

"Well, we don't need to keep it," says Phoebe.

"No—we're going to save that one," says Lawrence. "There's something worth saving on every one."

Phoebe sings the song through again. Then again. Once, she breaks off in the middle for no reason and giggles. Once, she drops a line. Then she sings the song again.

"Phoebe, I think it's all great," says Lawrence, "but I don't like the ending much."

"Do you like the front?" says Phoebe.

"I like the front and the bridge very much," says Lawrence. "I think the front and the bridge are terrific."

A woman has been standing between Bob Liftin and Elliot Lawrence, holding a stopwatch and a clipboard. This is Pat Daniels, a senior copywriter at Ayer. "I want to time the next one," she says to Lawrence. "She's sneaking in a little hey-hey-hey just before the bridge, and I need to know if we have time for it."

"I like it," says Lawrence. "It could use a little hey-hey-hey."

"It's not a long spot," she says.

"O.K., let's time it," says Lawrence.

Phoebe runs it through again, and again. At one point, Bill Eaton goes back into the recording studio to confer briefly with Phoebe. Fred McClafferty and George Eversman are near the door of the control room, leaning against the wall. Jerry Pfiffner is on a chair in front of the console and close to the big glass panel. The others around the console are mainly Lawrence's assistants; also, seated on a bench in the back of the room are about a half-dozen pale, extremely relaxed young men and women, all in jeans and vests and with stringy hair, who are referred to as "the Phoebe Snow organization."

Now a door in the back of the control room opens, and a man in a business suit, carrying a briefcase, approaches the group around the console and stands quietly to one side of it as Phoebe sings the "Reach

Out" song still another time. This is Phil Shyposh, Long Lines advertising manager. "How's it going?" he says to George Eversman.

Eversman greets Shyposh warmly. "Hi, Phil. Glad you could make it. I think it's sounding good."

"Good beat," says Shyposh.

"Yes, it's a good beat," says Eversman.

Phoebe finishes the latest take and stands there behind the glass, looking expectantly at Elliot Lawrence.

"That was nice, Phoebe," says Lawrence.

"I might have been coming down a little too much," says Phoebe.

"No, it was nice, Phoebe. It was one we can save. Now we need to do the narration."

"Oh, God," says Phoebe.

"It'll be a snap," says Lawrence.

Pat Daniels now goes into the recording studio and hands Phoebe a piece of paper. On it are the spoken lines that Phoebe is supposed to record, which will bring the spot up to sixty seconds. Phoebe screws up her face and begins to read, with an effort: "No matter how far I travel—"

"Back up from the mike just a touch," says Lawrence.

"No matter how far I travel, I keep my family and friends close by. That's the beauty of a phone call—it lets you always be there," Phoebe reads. Then she says, "That doesn't sound right, does it?"

"Take it easy. You'll get it in a moment," says Lawrence.

Bill Eaton is standing next to Lawrence at the console. "She's going cold on the narration," he says.

Jerry Pfiffner has come over from his spot down near the glass. "She's tensing," he says. "She's losing the flow."

As Phoebe tries the narration again, her voice sounds cold and flat; in fact, it becomes colder and flatter each time she tries it.

"You're getting close," says Lawrence.

"I can sure sing better than I can talk," says Phoebe. She screws up her face once more and concentrates on the piece of paper in her hand and reads the lines again: "That's the beauty of a phone call—it lets you always be there."

"It's not very warm, is it?" says Phil Shyposh.

"She was very warm in the song," says Fred McClafferty.

"Yes, I heard the song," says Shyposh.

"Elliot, let's make a change," says Jerry Pfiffner. "Let's change the 'always' to 'really.' "

"You want to do that?" says Lawrence.

"We need the warmth," says Pfiffner. "Maybe the 'really' will give her something to play with."

Lawrence leaves the console and goes out the door and into the studio, where he tells Phoebe about the word change, and then he returns to his place next to Bob Liftin. "She liked the change," he says. "O.K., Bob, we'll go again." Then, to Phoebe: "O.K., Phoebe, whenever you're ready."

Phoebe now reads the line again, this time putting

a lot of emphasis on the "really," and it sounds much better, much more natural.

"A little more sincerity, Phoebe," says Lawrence into the mike.

"That's the beauty of a phone call—it lets you *really* be there," says Phoebe.

"We can always boost it," says Bob Liftin.

"I don't want to throw the balance out," says Lawrence.

"That's the beauty of a phone call—it lets you *really* be there," says Phoebe once again.

"That's good," says Lawrence.

"It could go a shade closer in the front," says Liftin. "I've got a hole on either side."

"Phoebe, a little closer in the front," says Lawrence.

"That's the beauty of a phone call—it lets you *really* be there," says Phoebe.

"That's it," says Lawrence.

"Sounds great," says Eversman.

"Sounds really good," says Phil Shyposh.

A Different Mystique

BILL EATON, WHO DID THE MUSICAL ARRANGEMENT
of the "Reach Out" theme song for Phoebe Snow's
radio spot, writes music mainly for commercials and
promotional spots; for example, he composed the
"You're Looking Good, America" promotional theme
for CBS. He has also produced a couple of disco rec-
ords for Columbia and Warners, and he wrote one of
the songs that were used in the movie *Saturday Night
Fever*. He is a light-skinned, open-faced black man in
his early forties, with a modest Afro and bushy side-
burns, and usually wears bluejeans and a gray sweat-
shirt. This is what he says about his work on the
Phoebe Snow arrangement: "I took the original David
Lucas score and mulled it around in my head until I
reached a point of view. What I wanted was something
with a rock beat—but not too much of a rock beat—
and also with a hint of disco. I guess I mulled it
around in my head for about three days—I mean,

thinking about it while I was doing other things, and sometimes just thinking about it alone—but once I was satisfied that I'd committed myself to a point of view, then the rest was easy. When I do a commercial, I have to accept the responsibility for making it stylistically right for the artist, and for making it unique in such a way that the artist can convey his own personality. My work is *close* to popular, of course, but it's not the same as popular. It's hard to say just why, but I guess each form has its different mystique. You could probably say that my aim is always to produce a sound that is psychologically satisfying."

The Console

BOB LIFTIN TALKS ABOUT HIS MIXING-AND-RECORDing console, which he identifies as an MCI-500. "To begin with, you have two basic levels of measurement —V.U. and peak. V.U. is the average level, with very slow ballistics—meaning it doesn't register in instantaneous, short sound-pressure levels. The peak meter shows instantaneous levels and relates directly to what you hear. On the Snow recording, we used seventeen tracks just for the instruments. We brought the musicians in earlier in the morning and they laid down their tracks. We have five tracks just for drums. There's much more perfection in the system now, much more quality. I mean, with multiple tracking you can go right into the track; you can punch in and replace anything you've already recorded. Of course, I can't do everything on the MCI-500. That's why I have this MQS computer console here—for storage and retrieval."

The Interconnect

PHIL SHYPOSH HAS WHAT ONE IMAGINES TO BE THE classic look of the successful mid-level American company man. He is in his late thirties, with slightly thinning blondish hair, a broad forehead, and a sturdily handsome face that expresses, variously, a certain gruff friendliness and a hardworking practicality. Shyposh is the transliteration of a Russian name; his paternal grandparents were immigrants from the Ukraine. Phil grew up in Pennsylvania, played high-school football, and was fullback on the team at Temple University, in Philadelphia. In fact, despite his eyeglasses, business suit, and briefcase, he retains the unmistakable air of a man who was a successful athlete in his youth. It is not so much a matter of sheer physical dimensions—for though Shyposh is a square-shouldered six-footer, he does not come close to the behemoth standards of most contemporary professionals—as perhaps a certain self-confidence that derives from (among other things) growing up as a youthful oak among his scrawny peers. Shyposh has been with A.T.&T. for sixteen years, most of that time with the public-relations division of the company, where, as advertising manager, he still is today. One of the idiosyncrasies of the Bell System is a policy—apparently it dates back to an early company president, Theodore N. Vail—that advertising should be considered an instrument not merely of the company's attempts to sell its services but also of its attempts to "relate to" (or deal politically with) the public. Indeed, it was Vail who, in 1908, while trying to enlarge the Bell companies' clientele of three million subscribers in the face of unsavory connotations of monopoly among citizens and legislators, employed none other than the N. W. Ayer agency, of Philadelphia (already known for having devised, in 1906, what was perhaps the nation's first institutional advertising campaign, for the Mutual Life Insurance Company), to work up, and place in such periodicals as *Collier's* and *The Literary Digest,* a series of full-page advertisements explaining the good intentions and the social benefits of Bell-company service, each advertisement featuring A.T.&T.'s then recently designed bell-shaped logo.

Phil Shyposh talks about cream-skimming and the Interconnect: "Frankly, we've had to face a certain amount of competition in the past few years, and our present emphasis on advertising, especially on television advertising, is certainly a direct result of this competition. You might say the problems really started for us with the so-called Carterfone decision, back in 1968. The Carterfone was a device manufactured by a little electronics outfit in Texas called the Carter Electronics Company, which enabled small businessmen and farmers and so forth to connect their private two-way-radio systems into the telephone lines. As it had before, the phone company prohibited this type of interconnection, but the Carterfone people brought suit against A.T.&T., and when the federal court referred the matter to the F.C.C. for decision, this time the Commission decided against A.T.&T. The situation was pictured, as I remember, rather as a battle between David and Goliath, between the big guy and the little guys who were clients of the Carter Electronics Company. In the original depositions before the Commission, there were dozens of statements from ordinary folk down there in Texas—I seem to recall a man called Lilly who owned a welding shop in Ozona, Texas, and who wanted to be able to talk on the phone from his welding shop both with the guys in his delivery trucks and with his customers. Well, the government gave the little guys a break in dealing with the all-powerful phone company, and you can certainly see the sense in that. But the way things have actually worked out is that all these other companies, some of them quite sizable companies indeed—not necessarily little guys at all—have stepped into the communications market and plugged into the telephone company's lines and started cream-skimming. There's no way to describe it except as cream-skimming. In other words, the Bell System maintains profitable, high-traffic trunk routes, such as between New York and Chicago or between Los Angeles and Dallas, but it has to average out those profits and rates with all its hundreds of low-traffic, less profitable routes, such as between New York and Fargo, North Dakota. What the new private-line groups can now do, however, is to plug into the best volume business they can find—say, Chicago–St. Louis—and undercut us with rates as low as they can get away with. In fact, just about any outfit can get together a few subscribers and then plug into our Long Lines and sell its own plug-in service. We call it the Interconnect—the practice of interconnection—and I have to admit that it's forced us to take a much more aggressive position in the marketplace."

Phil Shyposh talks about the philosophy of the campaign: "To begin with, what you have to remember about residence long-distance calling is that it's a discretionary purchase. By that I mean there's nothing about a telephone that compels a person to make a long-distance call; you could even say that it's a reorder every time. So, basically, we've been trying to focus on a user strategy that appeals to the people who are already comfortable making a long-distance call, people who already like to express themselves that way, people who look on long-distance as an easy, non-traumatic experience. You might say that our objective is to get medium and heavy phone users to use the phone more often. It isn't that we don't care about the light user or the non-user, but it's like the airline campaigns that are directed at the frequent flier, or the beer campaigns that are directed at the heavy beer drinker. I mean, you can talk all you want about going after the non-flier or the non-beer drinker, but it hardly ever happens. I mean, how can you build a strategy around negatives? Right now, we're aiming for a generally younger audience than before, somewhat upscale, higher- rather than lower-income, mobile and fairly extroverted—people who talk on the phone because it makes them feel good, people who are happy using the telephone, people who are *facile* on the telephone. Eighty per cent of our target audience is in the twenty-five-to-forty-nine age bracket, and the tilt is definitely toward the female, seeing that women initiate sixty per cent of all residence long-distance phone calls."

Phil Shyposh talks about objectives: "We're looking for long-distance to carry more and more of the revenue burden in the system. Last year, residence long-distance revenues, gross, were about nine billion three hundred million dollars, and we hope to use our advertising, especially the television commercials, to raise this by twelve to fifteen per cent each year. Twelve per cent comes out to an increase of roughly a billion. I figure we'll spend about eighteen million to buy time for some twenty television commercials this year, which prorates at around nine hundred thousand per commercial. It's a good media buy."

More Greenery, Less Garage

Early in May, Steve Horn returns from Florida, muttering about bad weather in the Sunshine State, various delays, and a recalcitrant child actor, and asks the Ayer people to come by for a meeting at five in the afternoon. Once again, the group assembles in Horn's basement conference room, whose oak table is once again laden with Perrier, soft drinks, fruit, and cheese. Horn, with his gray silk scarf around his neck, sits at the head of the table, eating grapes. Linda, as usual, is on his left, with a large accordion folder beside her that contains the files on various shooting locations: the files are ordinary manila folders whose inside surfaces are covered with Polaroid snapshots of locations—mainly interiors—with numerical information penciled in about light and exposure angles.

At the moment, a suburban-house folder is being passed around for consideration as one of the locations for the yoga vignette.

Steve says: "I like this house. It's a little upscale, but it photographs very well."

Gaston says: "We could do the white yoga here."

Linda says: "Wouldn't the black yoga be better?"

Jerry says: "I'm not sure it reads black."

Steve says: "Don't worry. We can fix the downstairs room like a black girl's apartment, whatever that is. You know, give it a condominium look."

Gaston is meanwhile looking through another house folder. "There's a nicer house here," he says.

Linda says: "That's the Zacharia house. We've used that a lot. I know it almost as well as I know my own house."

Jerry says: "We have a black scene, but I don't know if this looks like a black house, either."

Steve says: "Let's take a look. I like this house, too. This room here has a very nice quality of light."

Gaston says: "I think we could do the white yoga here."

Jerry says: "It's a good house, but it's awfully upscale."

Steve says: "You know what I could do in this house? I could do the kid tap dancing."

Linda says: "I thought we were going to do the tap dancing in the Lawrence house."

Steve says: "Well, that's a good one, too, but I like this one better. It says tap dancing to me."

Gaston and Jerry have been looking at still another folder, and now they pass it to Linda.

Linda says: "I know *this* house as well as I know my own house."

Steve says: "You say that about every house."

Linda says: "That's not true. Just this one and maybe a couple of others. This one is a real dirty, low-down house, but we can make it look young again."

Steve says: "We could put some frills around, right?"

Linda says: "We could clean it up."

Jerry says: "Where do we need a young house?"

Steve says: "I'd like a young house for the toothless kid, but I don't think this is it."

Gaston passes him another folder. "What about this for white yoga?"

Steve looks at it in silence for a moment. Then: "You know, I could make it rain there."

Gaston says: "I don't think we're utilizing rain."

Steve says: "But I can utilize it here. I love rain. Visually, it's one of the best things. We could do something very nice in soft focus."

Jerry says: "Not too soft."

Steve says: "I mean normal soft focus."

Linda says: "You don't want to make it look too period."

Steve says: "I wasn't talking about period, I was talking about soft focus. Normal soft focus, nothing special."

Gaston says: "Maybe we should talk about the backstage vignette."

Steve says: "Let's use the Beacon Theatre."

Linda says: "I think we used it on the Rhonda Fleming shot."

Alayne produces a folder from a pile in front of her and gives it to Steve.

Steve opens it and examines the pictures with an increasingly perplexed expression. "Hell, this isn't the Beacon, this is the Lotos Club."

Linda says: "I like the Lotos Club. Remember? We used it for Paine Webber."

Steve says: "But it's not a theater."

Now Alayne hands him the Beacon folder and takes back the Lotos Club.

"Here we are," he says. "This is old-timey as hell."

Jerry says: "Maybe we should go with it."

Linda says: "We were hoping for the City Center, but there's a ballet there."

Gaston says: "Does it bother you to go back to the same location?"

Steve says: "Nobody knows if you go back. Besides, I hardly ever shoot wide-angle."

Now the group turns to a discussion of race-track locations for the jockey vignette. In the course of the past ten days, Ray Guarino, Steve Horn's location scout, has been checking on race tracks within a hundred miles of New York and has brought back at least fifty different Polaroid views. But as soon as Jerry and Gaston start looking at them it is apparent that something is wrong.

Jerry says: "The problem I'm having with these locations is that they don't say race track to me, they say garage."

Ray says: "I Polaroided every track and paddock in the area."

Steve says: "I agree about this bunch, but I think we could use that area out at Roosevelt Raceway."

Gaston says: "If this is Roosevelt I'm looking at, it has an awful lot of concrete. It looks like a car-racing place."

Steve says: "A while ago, we shot a race-track thing for 7Up in California. We brought in all sorts of trees and grass to make it look right."

Jerry says: "I don't see how we can make Roosevelt look right."

Gaston says: "I'd say we need more greenery, less garage."

Ray says: "I think they're all like that. I checked out every track in the area."

Steve says: "Maybe we should check farther away. Maybe we should even cheat a little—you know, go for the greenery and prop the track effect."

Finally, there is a discussion of locations for the rodeo vignette, which Ray has been scouting in what might seem unlikely areas of New Jersey and Pennsylvania. The generally favored location is in New Jersey, but it apparently presents a difficulty.

Gaston says: "I think we have a phone problem."

Steve says: "What kind of a phone problem?"

Gaston says: "Well, this is a phone-company ad. We have to have a phone there somewhere."

Steve says: "Well, we can just put one in, like we do everywhere else."

Linda says: "The point is, you can't just put a phone *anywhere* in a rodeo corral."

Steve says: "Well, I didn't mean we'd put it *anywhere*. We could stick a phone on one of the posts."

Linda says: "What's a phone doing on a post?"

Jerry says: "I don't think the phone problem is going to be so hard to solve. I think our main problem is getting a place that says rodeo."

Steve says: "Yes, we have to be careful it doesn't say farm."

Jerry says: "Something rustic and rundown."

Steve says: "Definitely not farm."

Gaston says: "So where do we put the phone?"

Jerry says: "The phone problem isn't major. Trust me."

Our Team

STEVE HORN, ALAYNE BAXTER, AND JOANNA DEN-
del discuss costumes for the hockey-player vignette.
Joanna Dendel is a dark-haired woman in her early
thirties who once worked at Bonwit Teller and now
free-lances as a wardrobe mistress, or what today is
known in the business as a stylist.

Alayne says: "It's in a locker room, isn't it? So you
could have some bare skin."

Steve says: "Look, it's the phone company. We don't
want nudity."

Alayne says: "We could have shoulder pads, then."

Joanna says: "It seems to me they wear underwear
—you know, long johns. They cut them off around the
legs."

Alayne says: "You mean we'd have a scene full of
underwear?"

Joanna says: "Frankly, I don't think underwear is

the problem. I think the shirt emblem is the problem."

Steve says: "That's sharp thinking, Joanna. We've definitely got to work out the emblem. We need a *generic* emblem. I mean, we can't just put anything on that shirt, because maybe it'll be the emblem of some real team."

Joanna says: "How about a pair of hockey sticks?"

Steve says: "Have you checked it out?"

Joanna says: "No, I just thought of it."

Steve says: "Well, you have to check it out. I mean, you can't just put a pair of hockey sticks on a hockey shirt. That wouldn't be generic."

Joanna says: "How about an animal head? A lion or a bear."

Steve says: "Nobody ever heard of a lion or bear hockey team."

Joanna says: "So then it's generic."

Steve says: "Generic isn't everything. A lion or bear doesn't look right."

Alayne says: "They have lions and bears in football."

Steve says: "That's what I mean. A lion or bear isn't hockey."

Joanna says: "There are other animals besides lions and bears."

Steve says: "Yes, but they all look like something that's being used. I mean, an eagle is good—right—but it looks like a Black Hawk. We need something special, something distinctive, something that says this is our team."

Alayne says: "Our team?"

Steve says: "Sure. Who else's team?"

Italians Make Good Cowboys

STEVE HORN, LINDA HORN, AND JERRY, GASTON, and Elliott discuss final casting for the rodeo vignette. On the production sheet, under "Vignette" it says "Rodeo"; under "Location Description" it says "Somewhere in the barn, stable, or tunnel behind paddock area. See horses, trailers, rodeo clown, etc."; under "Wardrobe" it says "Cowboy getup with hat, jeans, boots, spurs, etc., number on back and chest, and looking a little the worse for wear"; and under "Cast" it says "Guy in his early twenties, plus ten extras." The group has reassembled in Steve Horn's conference room, this time to watch another batch of videotaped auditions. These are the "callbacks": the finalists, who have already been seen once by the Horns and the Ayer people, and have been marked "maybe." They were called back for a second audition the day before. Today the group is casting only the principal: the cowboy; the ten extras will be sent out by the agencies on the day of the shooting, like a bulk order.

On the black-and-white TV screen, a variety of cowboy types make their appearance. Some are large and jolly; some are tall and thin. Some are clearly too old for the part; some are too stiff or uncertain. For this second audition, most of the actors have tried to dress for the role, wearing bluejeans and Western-style shirts and, in many cases, cowboy boots and cowboy hats; and something that is noticeable—and surprising —is how authentic most of them appear. On the little screen, as they step into camera range to begin the videotaped audition—eyes straight ahead, arms at sides, no particular expression on the face beneath the cowboy hat—each man looks like a cowboy; or, rather, he looks like what one is accustomed to seeing on the movie or TV screen as a cowboy. But then as the audition begins, and the actor—telephone to his ear—is required to simulate the aw-shucks pleasure of a cowboy talking on the phone to his jockey girlfriend (at the race track that Ray has been trying to locate) , in most instances the cowboy look disintegrates into cuteness and occasionally into giggles.

A cowboy-garbed actor, clearly in his thirties, now steps into view.

Elliott says: "That's a macho Western look, all right."

Linda says: "He's Italian, that's why. Italians make good cowboys."

Jerry says: "He's too old."

The Italian cowboy does his stint on the telephone and then leaves, to be replaced by a nearly opposite type: short, blond, and boyish.

Linda says: "I like this one a lot. He's kind of like the baseball player in the Sony ad."

Steve says: "He's more like the guy in the Foamy ad."

Linda says: "They're both the same guy—didn't you know?"

The blond cowboy pulls out all the stops in the telephone scene. "Hi, *sugar,* ain't you the *sweetest* chick? Did you really *win* that race? Boy, ain't you *somethin'?* Boy, do I *miss* you," he improvises.

Jerry says: "Too many dimples."

Linda says: "But he's cute, isn't he?"

Steve says: "I don't mind the dimples if we can get the lighting right, but we can do better."

They see about eight more cowboys, most of them of the blond and cute variety, though a couple are closer to the good-ole-boy type, with big bellies and a certain down-home look. One, in particular, has a nice, friendly, grainy face that doesn't collapse during the telephone scene.

Jerry says: "He might do."

Steve says: "He's too Southern."

Linda says: "He's from Jackson Heights."

Steve says: "I mean, he looks Southern. He says barnyard to me."

Linda says: "I'll bet he'd be surprised to know that."

Finally, toward the end of the tape, what seems to

be a compromise candidate turns up. His name is Preston Brown. He is tall, blondish, not too old, not too young, not too cute, not too Sicilian or too farmer-like.

Jerry says: "He's not John Wayne, but he holds the look."

Steve says: "Don't you think he could ride a horse?"

Gaston says: "He doesn't have to ride a horse."

Steve says: "No, but he looks like he could ride one if he had to."

The Client Meeting

AT THE START OF THE SECOND WEEK IN MAY, AN event known as the Client Meeting takes place. Once again, the Horn and Ayer people assemble in Steve Horn's conference room, but at this meeting there are some additions to the usual gathering: the client, A.T.&T., is represented by Phil Shyposh and his assistant, Mac McDaniel, and the N. W. Ayer agency is represented by (in addition to the Creative Group of Jerry, Gaston, and Elliott) the Account Group of George Eversman, Fred McClafferty, and Buzz Sawyer. Thus, there are more than a dozen men and women (the only women this time being Linda Horn and Alayne Baxter) seated around the big conference table, whose centerpiece of food and drink has been augmented by a pot of espresso coffee and a plate of little cakes.

The purpose of the meeting is to present the final

shooting arrangements (which Steve Horn and the Ayer creative people have been working out together, by conference and phone call, over the past two weeks) for the approval of the client, and so, from the start, the meeting takes on an at least superficially business-like tone. Jerry Pfiffner introduces the Horns to Shyposh and McDaniel, and also introduces the Horns to the three Ayer account men. Gaston Braun distributes an elegantly typed and bound copy of the shooting arrangements to the participants. There are modest, not altogether insincere conversations about traffic problems, for both Shyposh and McDaniel have driven into the city from Long Line headquarters, in Bedminster, New Jersey, and Jerry Pfiffner takes a bus in to work each morning from New Jersey. Linda Horn offers coffee to McClafferty and Eversman, who are on her left, and then discovers that there are no coffee cups. Alayne is dispatched to find the maid, and the maid brings in a tray of coffee mugs. "They're the wrong kind," Linda says, then thinks better of it. The maid leaves the tray, with a shrug, and teeters off.

Something that is noticeable at this meeting is the different kinds of clothing worn by the men. The Ayer creative people, for example, have remained relatively true to their informal, urban-bohemian garb: Jerry and Gaston are both wearing bluejeans and sports shirts, while Elliott, a Long Island commuter, wears a pair of light-brown slacks, an open-necked shirt, and a sweater. The account people and client people, however, are clearly costumed as businessmen, though with subtle hierarchical gradations in dress, which are perhaps a result of different salary levels: Phil Shyposh wears a handsome, conservative gabardine suit, while his assistant, McDaniel, wears a dark-blue leisure suit; comparably, both Eversman and McClafferty wear sedate well-tailored gray plaid suits, while Buzz Sawyer, who is junior to them, wears a light-blue leisure suit. Steve Horn himself seems to have attempted a compromise between the uniforms of art and business, for although he has abandoned his Western look for a suit, the suit he has chosen is decidedly raffish, or at least European, in cut—at any rate, not markedly businesslike—and with it he sports a white shirt and a brown silk necktie, complete with tiepin, and also a brown silk scarf, loosely knotted.

As the mugs of espresso are being passed, Gaston opens the proceedings, speaking from his seat, between Jerry and Elliott, and assuming a methodical and strangely pompous manner, which doubtless indicates the business-oriented tilt of the assembly. "My view is that we should start the meeting by reviewing the production schedule," he says. "Then we should review the casting choices that have been made and the locations that have been selected. I think we should review all phases of the operation as they pertain to the over-all schedule."

Eversman says: "What about the music?"

Elliott says: "We're still working on demos."

Jerry says: "This way, we have the flexibility of bounce-back."

63

McClafferty says: "Are we going to need a lot of bounce-back?"

Jerry says: "We need the flexibility."

Gaston then turns the meeting over to Steve Horn, who tries to describe the various scenes, or vignettes, he will be filming. For example: "O.K., now, our first vignette here starts backstage. We've got this man who's a professional entertainer—his name is Paul Reed. We're going to try to shoot at the Beacon Theatre. It's a good theater, with a good backstage look—I think you'll like it. We'll have the guy in a white-tie getup, and he'll do his tap-dance routine. We'll also have a lot of special color in the background —lots of chorus girls. It'll look like a real production— a real bustling scene." As Horn describes the successive vignettes, it is clear that these are essentially *his* scenes—that he has taken charge of the production.

As each vignette is described, Linda or Gaston passes around a Polaroid snapshot of its principal actors to the account people and the client people, who for the most part confine their comments to murmured agreement, interrupted only now and then by modest questioning, somewhat in the manner of dinner guests who have been invited to attend the host's slide-show lecture on Yellowstone Park and feel they should ask occasional questions, in a tactful manner, so as to make a visible display of alertness and involvement. Thus, after Horn describes the soldier-in-the-barracks vignette, which has been shifted from the reluctant military academies to an abandoned Army base, Linda passes along to McClafferty a snapshot of the actor who will play the soldier.

Linda says: "He's very cute, don't you think?"

McClafferty says: "Yes, he is."

Steve says: "He's a really terrific actor. I think you're all going to like him a lot."

Linda says: "He's going to go and get all his hair cut off just for us."

Shyposh says: "You mean he's going to get his hair cut down to regulation length?"

Steve says: "He's a very good actor. He's gonna do whatever he has to."

Eversman says: "That means really short, you know. Not just a crewcut."

Shyposh says: "Well, now, I'm wondering—are we sure it's not going to be too shiny?"

Steve says: "No, it's not going to be shiny."

McClafferty says: "It seems to me those military barbers usually leave a little fringe."

Shyposh says: "I don't think we want something too shiny."

Steve says: "It's not going to be *bald*. I don't like bald."

McDaniel says: "Too bald can be distracting."

Steve says: "Absolutely."

Gaston says: "Before we move on, I think we ought to talk a little about the uniforms."

Steve says: "I thought we were decided."

Gaston says: "No, we're still undecided."

Steve says: "I thought we were going with camouflage."

Jerry says: "We might go with camouflage. But we might have to go with green."

Eversman says: "If the guy is a Marine, all Marine uniforms are now camouflage."

Gaston says: "Do you know that for a fact?"

Eversman says: "Well, I'd bet on it."

Steve says: "Then I guess that's set. We go with camouflage."

A few other continuing problems are brought up and either solved or partly solved. For example, in the yoga vignette:

Linda says: "We've added a baby to the white girl. We looked at it and we thought, We have no baby anywhere. So we added a baby."

Gaston says: "A baby is always nice."

Shyposh says: "What about the black girl? How do we balance with the black girl?"

Steve says: "With the black girl, the way we're thinking is that a cat walks by."

McClafferty says: "That's good. That's a good effect."

Steve says: "I mean, you can't have both girls just standing upside down. Our thinking is we use a couple of little human touches, the baby and the cat, and we give the thing that little spark."

There is also the question of whom to cast as the

hockey player whose teeth are missing, in the hockey vignette.

Steve says: "We've had a lot of trouble with this one."

Shyposh says: "You mean there aren't any actors with missing teeth?"

Steve says: "No, there are plenty of actors with missing teeth. There just aren't any actors who want to appear on TV with missing teeth."

Eversman says: "What about a professional?"

Steve says: "That's where we're looking. We might get Bobby Clarke, if he's not busy."

Jerry says: "Bobby Clarke is definitely toothless."

Shyposh says: "How many teeth do we need missing?"

Steve says: "All we need is two. Maybe three. But two would be fine. Two would give us the look."

Finally, there is the matter of the telephone in the rodeo vignette.

Gaston says: "All right, we have to resolve this situation. What kind of phone do we want?"

Linda says: "Red."

Steve says: "I think we should have a red desk phone."

Gaston says: "I was thinking wall phone."

Linda says: "You don't want a desk phone at a rodeo."

Elliott says: "Wall or desk, I don't see it makes much difference."

McClafferty says: "Maybe we want to use a Trim-line there?"

Jerry says: "I like Trimlines, except we tested them and they really wipe out the face."

Shyposh says: "I wonder if we don't want a more prominent telephone."

Gaston says: "For a while, I was thinking booths."

McDaniel says: "Booths don't seem very friendly."

Steve says: "What about rotary dial? Rotary dial gives you that old-time feeling."

Eversman says: "I don't know about rotary dial. I was thinking more Touch Tone."

McClafferty says: "Touch Tone is definitely prominent."

Jerry says: "We could go with a black Touch Tone. I mean, it's a stable situation."

Gaston says: "No wipeout?"

Linda says: "Steve can handle the wipeout."

Steve says: "I don't see any problem, except where to put it."

Jerry says: "There's always a place to put a phone in at a rodeo."

The Script

T HIS IS THE SHOOTING SCRIPT FOR "TAP DANCING"
that was approved at the Client Meeting:

CLIENT: AT&T LONG LINES
PRODUCT: LONG DISTANCE
TITLE: "TAP DANCING"
FACILITIES: TV
DATE: MAY 7, 1979
LENGTH: 30

VIDEO

1. Open on older man in a "show-biz" setting.
(Backstage, dressing room, rehearsal hall, whatever.) He's standing while listening, perhaps with
his eyes closed, on phone.

2. Cut to living-room scene with the corner of
the rug thrown back. Little girl is tap dancing with

shiny new tap shoes. Proud father holds phone down near tapping as mother beams proudly.

3. Cut back to elderly man as he smiles more widely and begins to impulsively dance to the same step himself.

4. Cut to brand-new Army recruit with brand-new short haircut. He's rubbing his head.

5. Cut to barber friend or dad sitting in his own barber chair, laughing.

6. Cut to gal standing on head in yoga position. She's on phone.

7. Cut to another gal doing the same.

8. Cut to young man in cowboy getup—hat, jeans, etc. He has just competed in a rodeo, still has number on back and chest and is a little the worse for wear. He's somewhere in the barn, stable, behind-the-scenes area. He's on the phone and happy. We see horses, trailers, maybe a rodeo clown, etc.

9. Cut to young woman in jockey outfit just fresh from the race. She's full of mud. She's talking very happily on the phone.

10. Cut to locker room with hockey player waiting on phone. Lots of bustling around him.

11. Cut to toothless little boy on phone in same uniform, whooping it up.

12. Cut back to locker room as champagne is poured over his head and he breaks into a big toothless smile. Freeze on smile. Mortise. Super and logo.

Kind of Family

THE FIRST DAY OF SHOOTING IS A HOT, SUNNY MAY morning, and by eight-thirty, after a forty-minute drive from the city, the Steve Horn film crew is setting up equipment inside the Dambach house in Wyckoff, New Jersey. From the quiet, tree-lined street—virtually bereft of traffic, since the neighborhood commuters have apparently already departed for their offices —the Dambach house appears to be an unusually handsome old fashioned edifice of sandstone; indeed, on a well near the front door there is a small signboard inscribed "Circa 1770." Thus, we are apparently in the presence of pre-Revolutionary architecture. More immediately, though, we are in the presence of contemporary filmmaking. A number of miscellaneous vehicles are parked along the Dambachs' driveway and on the lawn: many cars; a couple of vans; two small trucks; one large white truck, from which lights and camera apparatus are being unloaded and carried inside the house. Young men, some of them in T-shirts, some bare-chested, march into the house carrying pieces of equipment; they are union hands—grips, props, and gaffers—hired, variously, for the day or for the whole project. A maze of thick black cables threads past one of the small trucks and along a brick walkway, and disappears through the front door. Inside the Dambach house, there obtains a not uncheerful atmosphere of generally controlled confusion. Steve Horn, wearing carpenter pants, a khaki-colored T-shirt, no scarf, and a sort of baseball cap turned backward on his head, like a catcher's, stands in a corner of the living room directing the removal of a pink armchair. One of his assistants, Vincent Donohue, wearing a panama hat and with a cigarette in his mouth, is taking light-level readings. The assistant cameraman, Loet Farkas, is working on the positioning of a camera, which is now just inside the doorway to the room, looming between an old table and a Victorian standing lamp like an eccentric addition to the room's sedate furnishings. Alayne Baxter is laying down a white dropcloth on part of the floor. Gaston Braun and Linda Horn are attempting to shift a baby-grand piano away from the wall. The crew members move in and out of the rooms, which seem now to be entirely threaded with cables. Out in the back yard, the assistant director, Ron Palazzo, supervises the setting of tables with coffee, boxes of doughnuts and bagels, some soft drinks, and a platter of what appear to be canapés—pieces of ham and pineapple affixed to little toothpicks. Out in the front yard, Jerry Pfiffner and Elliott Manketo are looking over the shoulders of a young man called Danny, who is seated on a chair and is operating a videotape-playback machine that has been set up on a table on the lawn. On its little TV screen, connected by still more cables to a 35-mm. movie camera inside, can be seen a TV image identical to what the main camera is focussed on: right now, Gaston Braun rearranging a piano stool. Inside, Barbara, the script girl, sits on the hall staircase writing in a loose-leaf notebook. Two men appear at the front door, pushing a rack of clothes, and ask for wardrobe. Wardrobe is out in back; also makeup. Mac McDaniel, from A.T.&T. Long Lines, ambles into the house and asks how things are going. "They're going great," says Vincent.

On the back porch sit the three actors in the second "Tap Dancing" vignette. (As in most film work, the scenes are being shot out of sequence.) These are Linda Swenson, who plays the mother; James O'Sullivan, who plays the father; and Tiffany Blake, who plays the little girl tap dancer, and who is accompanied by her actual mother. O'Sullivan sits at one end of a couch reading *The Wall Street Journal*. Linda Swenson is across the porch being made up by the makeup man, Richard Hartenstein. Tiffany Blake stands still to have her red-white-and-blue dancing dress pinned by Joanna Dendel and meanwhile dabs at a coloring book with a couple of crayons.

Tiffany's mother is Mrs. David Ganz. A friendly,

ample woman in her mid-thirties, she is seated at the far end of the couch from O'Sullivan, and is holding in one hand a copy of Tiffany's work contract and in the other hand a box of crayons. "Tiffany's only seven, but she's been very active," Mrs. Ganz says. "Last fall, she was in *Annie* for a couple of months. Recently, she did a Jell-O Pudding commercial. She also did something for AMF Bowling. Then, just a few months ago, we went to Japan for the Taiyo Fishery Company. Tiffany was one of a group of seven kids—seven kids chosen out of at least seven hundred! I have to tell you, the Taiyo Fishery people treated us very nicely. I mean, it was a definitely first-class operation. They'd built this huge tuna can—I mean, really huge, like an oil-storage tank—and the seven kids danced around on top of it. The can revolved, too, so the kids danced as it revolved. Tiffany signed a three-year contract with Taiyo, with the understanding that Tiffany only goes back when she's not busy. After all, she has her schoolwork to think of, doesn't she? Schoolwork is important at her age. That's something we've always been very serious about: keeping up with schoolwork. Tiffany goes to Magnolia Open School, out in Long Beach, Long Island, next to Lido Beach, where we live, and she's always right near the top of the class. She's a smart kid, all right, but very unpretentious. The way I see it, these commercials are wonderful experience—I mean, think of seeing Japan at seven years old—and also they're going to earn her money for college. I take her to auditions two or three times a week—well, sometimes more and sometimes less. It can be a long ride in from Lido Beach, especially in winter, but now the agencies call her, and who am I to stand in the kid's way?"

It has been nearly two hours since the crew started setting up, and now, around ten-thirty, there are indications from within that Steve Horn is ready to begin filming. The three principals troop to the living room (which is encircled with lights and reflectors), and Steve arranges them in position: O'Sullivan is asked to crouch down at the foot of the piano; Linda is seated at the piano, as if playing it; Tiffany stands between the two and practices her tapping.

Steve says: "O.K., James, you're gonna be talking on the phone to your father, who's a professional entertainer. Now, you're *talking* and you're *looking,* and your *eyes* are on your little girl. O.K., Tiffany, the important thing is never, never look at me."

One of the crew hands O'Sullivan a Trimline phone to practice with.

Gaston says: "Do you think he should hold it out so far?"

Steve says: "I think it's O.K., but the background's too dark."

Vincent says: "The problem is with the stairway."

Steve says: "The rug should roll away from the daddy."

A couple of men kneel down and roll the rug away from O'Sullivan.

Steve says: "Are we ready?"

Linda Horn says: "The little girl has too much perspiration."

Richard Hartenstein darts out with his makeup kit and removes the drops of sweat.

Jerry says: "Wouldn't we be better off with a regular phone? I've been watching it on the videotape, and I don't think it reads this way."

Gaston says: "We might as well try it this way."

Steve says: "Are we ready? All right."

The script girl, Barbara, walks in front of Tiffany, holding up a board that says "Production No. AXLL9313, AT&T, Scene 202, Take 1," and then steps back.

"Camera," says Steve. "Take One."

Since all the vignettes in the "Tap Dancing" commercial will be silent (that is, without dialogue) except for new "Reach Out" music and lyrics, which will be put in when all the filming is done, the on-the-spot effect of the actors' spoken performance is strangely amateurish and haphazard, in some ways like an unusually elaborate home movie—for though none of the actors' words are being recorded, the actors all speak to each other as the camera runs, sometimes improvising dialogue, at other times urging each other on. Thus, when the action starts, Linda Swenson begins an elementary version of "Ain't She Sweet?" on the piano as Tiffany launches into her little tap dance, and O'Sullivan, seated on the floor, alternately burbles into the telephone and brandishes it in the direction of Tiffany's tapping shoes. "O.K., Dad, now listen to this!" he exclaims. "Isn't that great? Isn't she some dancer? You're doing great, honey. Just keep on dancin' for old Dad. Just keep on moving them feet. Oh, yes, I bet you're loving that, Dad. I bet it's getting to you." Nor is Linda Swenson silent during her piano routine, for as she plays she repeatedly turns toward Tiffany, beaming enthusiastically and declaiming, "Oh, that's so good, honey. That's really good. That's just great." When the take is over, the two adult actors, as if exhausted from so much hyperbole, lapse into a relatively somber silence.

Steve says: "Not bad. We need it looser."

They do another take; also a third.

Steve says: "I have an inspiration. I want the daddy to have that hat." The hat is a red cardboard object —an item discarded from Tiffany's costume, which is a relic from the old musical comedy *Gypsy*. The hat is now handed to O'Sullivan. "James, suppose you try playing with that hat. No, I don't mean twirling. Nothing too extreme. Maybe something back and forth. Maybe holding it by the rim. No, that's too much twirling. Yes, that's it. Something *natural*. All right. Are we ready? Camera. Take Four."

O'Sullivan now does his talking-to-Dad routine holding the little red cardboard hat in his free hand.

When it's over, Steve says: "Too much twirling. More back and forth."

They do it again.

Steve says: "The hat is getting better."

Elliott comes in and says: "I have to tell you, the videotape doesn't pick up the phone."

Jerry also appears, and says: "Everybody's doing something. Dancing. Waving a hat. But we don't see the phone. It doesn't read."

Gaston says: "Maybe we should use the regular phone. It reads faster."

Steve says: "O.K. with me."

A member of the crew brings in the new phone, and they do another take.

Elliott reports in from the videotape machine on the lawn: "The new phone reads a lot better."

Steve says: "Ron, I'm wondering, are we too far away with the light?"

Ron Palazzo says: "Which way too far?"

Steve says: "Let's move that 4-K in a foot."

A couple of men move one of the big lights a foot closer to the piano.

Steve begins another take but stops in mid-flow.

Steve says: "Tiffany, you're looking."

Tiffany says: "I didn't know I was looking."

Steve says: "You were looking."

Another take.

Steve says: "Tiffany, don't look here at all."

Another take.

Steve says: "Tiffany, please don't look at me."

Another take.

Steve says: "I want the daddy to keep the hat still."

O'Sullivan says: "I can skip the hat."

Steve says: "No, I want the hat. But not so much activity."

O'Sullivan says: "No back and forth?"

Steve says: "No back and forth."

Another take.

Steve says: "Tiffany, you were looking at me."

Tiffany says: "I wasn't."

Another take.

Steve says: "All right, that's it. I have to tell you, that was a really cute scene."

As the crew begins to strike the set, and Steve, Jerry, and Gaston are standing together in the disarray of the room, a woman in a dark-blue dress, who has been hovering on the edges of the proceedings since early morning, often with camera in hand, now approaches the three and snaps their picture. This is Mrs. Kenneth Dambach, whose house it is. Afterward, she approaches Mac McDaniel, of A.T.&T., who has also been keeping to the sidelines most of the day.

"It's been very exciting," she says, introducing herself.

"It's certainly a lovely home," says McDaniel, stepping out of the way as one of the big 4-K lights is trundled by him.

"Yes, we like it," says Mrs. Dambach. "And we always like having Steve and Linda. You know, they did Avon here a few months ago. By now, we think of them as kind of family."

Really Pretty People

ON THEIR WAY BACK INTO THE CITY IN THE "TALent van," Linda Swenson and James O'Sullivan (who met for the first time on this filming) discuss working with Steve Horn and various aspects of their craft.

Linda Swenson says: "Technically, Steve frames shots as beautifully as anyone, and he lights them terrifically well. Also, he has a concept that's very human. He isn't afraid to deal in human emotions."

James O'Sullivan says: "I feel comfortable working with Steve, because I know the commercial is going to get on the air. A lot of directors you work with, you get the feeling that they don't really know what they're doing and that you're wasting your time. I mean, you bust your ass all day and nothing ever comes of it. Steve's very good technically and very good on preparation. You don't mind busting your ass for him, because you know it's going to work out."

Linda Swenson says: "The thing is, Steve really cares, and I think the results show in his work."

James O'Sullivan says: "Definitely. He's very committed. Also, he's good at protecting his actors. On some other directors' sets, you always have a whole bunch of client people and account people buzzing around and telling you what to do and what not to do. It's very hard on actors. It distracts you from your work."

Linda Swenson says: "Steve always gets the best out of his actors."

James O'Sullivan says: "He definitely protects you. And, frankly, this is not a branch of the acting business where the actor is in a seller's market, if you know what I mean. My experience, lately, has been that more and more models are showing up for auditions. I'm talking about male models. For the most part, these are guys with only flat-work experience, and I have to tell you they make me angry, because most of them can hardly say three words out loud. But I guess the model agencies are pushing them. I even heard that some of the agencies were trying to give their guys acting lessons. But it's hard on the working actor. Only the other day, I walked in for an audition and I honestly felt ugly. I mean, there were all these really pretty people sitting around, and I mean *really pretty,* and even though most of them couldn't cut it workwise, I have to tell you, I felt out of place."

Linda Swenson says: "I find you run into most of the model types out in California. When I first started in commercial work, just about everything was being done in New York, but in the last few years I think the balance has shifted a little. A lot of the actors I know work New York from spring to October; then, when the weather changes and the shooting moves to the Coast, they move with it. But I think some of those production people out there are gonna have to change their act. Like, out there, the casting guys call you at six in the evening for a shoot scheduled for the next morning. Out there, they work weekends. They work any time they feel like it. It's not businesslike in California. They don't have outfits like Steve Horn. Of course, what they do have is a whole lot of gorgeous people. I mean, in the East you got character, but out there in California you've got a whole lot of *looks*."

James O'Sullivan says: "I think things started coming together for me in the business when I began figuring out what they wanted. I mean, I've been doing well financially for the past six years, because I've been doing soaps, and the past two years have been really good, because I've been playing Jeff Martin in *All My Children*. But you can't count on something like that going on forever, right? So it's important, careerwise, to build yourself up in commercials. I've done Head & Shoulders. I've done Bold. I've done One-A-Day vitamins. From a career perspective, I want to do more. But you got to be smart in this business. I mean, you can't just go in there and take what they throw at you, because a lot of the time they don't know what they want. I remember once auditioning for an aspirin commercial and the casting guy says, 'Hey, now, we want happiness, we want joy, we want you to be all fired up!' I thought to myself, Probably one of the top agency guys has said to the casting guy, 'Give me some energy and drive,' and the casting guy thinks energy and drive means happiness. But who wants *happiness* on an aspirin commercial? I mean, you have to use your brains in this business; you can't let the flow roll over you. I try to study commercials on the TV when I'm home—you know, learn from them. I mean, there are a million things to learn. But the trouble is I really don't like commercials. I kind of hate them. I mean, some days I get up and go on a call, and when I walk in that room I just can't stand it."

Linda Swenson says: "No kidding? I really don't feel that way about it at all. I love the work."

James O'Sullivan says: "Don't get me wrong. I always give it my best shot."

Linda Swenson says: "Actually, I have a Master of Fine Arts from Columbia and trained as a serious actress. I've been in a couple of Off Broadway plays. Last year, I was in a production of *The Hostage* in Rochester. But I really love commercial work. I've done Campbell's soups, Kodak, Joy detergent. I guess I've done a lot of main-line products because I have a kind of main-line look. I think what I like best is the feeling you have of communicating with all those people out there."

James O'Sullivan says: "And the money?"

Linda Swenson says: "The money is important, but I wouldn't want to do the work if the feeling wasn't right. I'll tell you what I hate, though. I hate those commercials where you have to eat things. Once, I remember, we were doing this job for McDonald's. We'd taken over one of their shops and we'd started real early in the morning, and the place was just crawling with agency people and client people and production people, and I was supposed to eat this *one* hamburger. All I had to take was a couple of bites, but something always seemed to go wrong—sometimes with the lighting, sometimes with the hamburger—and the hours went by and they kept giving me hamburger after hamburger. Each one, of course, was stone cold, since they hold together better that way; and each one was coated with grease—I mean, really coated with grease—because they're supposed to photograph better that way. By the end of the day, I reckoned I'd chomped away on fifty stone-cold, greasy hamburgers, flashing this big happy smile each time, and, I'm telling you, that may not be Shakespeare but it sure was acting."

Billy's Rain

THE DAY IS COOL AND OVERCAST, WITH WHAT THE
radio announcers are gravely calling the threat of
rain, though since the city sidewalks seem to be still
warm and laden with the dust and debris from the
steamy day before, it is hard to regard the threat as
especially menacing. Moreover, the day has not yet
properly begun, for it is only six-thirty, and the city is
mostly quiet. Perhaps it is not exactly asleep, for it is
well known to be a city of insomniacs, but, except for
an occasional newspaper truck or solitary, mysteriously
speeding taxi or equally solitary, loping jogger (and,
of course, radio announcers), the streets and avenues
are generally still, even hushed (possibly in forebod-
ing of the threat of rain), and are certainly without
their typical noisy communal activity—except for East
Fifty-fourth Street, just off First Avenue, where a big
white truck is double-parked, also four vans and several cars, as the Steve Horn crew loads huge lights, and

several dozen metal cases of camera equipment, and little lights, and reflector shields, and rolls of cable, and electrical connections, and videotape equipment, and wardrobe racks, and coffee urns, and now two ladders, and now three large multicolored umbrellas, and now an ice chest full of Perrier and Dr Pepper. All these items are being disgorged through the dark-green garage door and then rolled, carried, hauled, or shoved into the various vehicles. The effect is somewhat like that of a large and eccentric (and clearly photo-oriented) family about to embark on an outing in the country and not able to quite agree on what to take—or even more like that of a reunion of old Army buddies, for half the men on the sidewalk are wearing military jackets of one sort or another, while the remainder (mostly the more youthful members of the group) wear little more than undershirts (above their jeans) in which to greet the chill dawn air. There is much clatter and chat between the garage door and the street, a good part of it coming from a walkie-talkie carried by Vincent, which emits random, high-volume bursts of static, and with which he is apparently trying to communicate with Ron Palazzo, some thirty feet away but inside and below street level, in the Steve Horn office.

There, downstairs, a different sort of activity is taking place—less military and more white-collar. Two secretaries are typing. Linda Horn is checking some wardrobe details with Joanna. Alayne is on the telephone. Ron Palazzo is leaning against a bulletin board (on which are pinned a couple of schedule sheets for the recently completed Coke shoot and numerous vacation postcards from the staff) and trying to write on his clipboard with one hand while working his walkie-talkie with the other. "I can hear you," he says, "but only every third word. *Third* word."

Just then, a pretty black girl comes down the stairs, looks around her, and spies a blond white girl (nice-looking but not as pretty) sitting on one of the wood benches.

"Hi," she says brightly to the blond girl, who looks up sleepily and smiles. "Did you see me in the Pepsi?"

"I was in Florida," the blond girl says. "Was it national?"

"Of course it was national," the black girl says. Then, to Palazzo: "Do you have a sign-in sheet?"

Palazzo says: "We don't use sign-in sheets here. We're very loose."

Steve Horn appears from down the corridor, followed by an older, gray-haired man in a business suit who is carrying an oil painting of a woman's face. The older man sets the painting down on the floor, leaning against the wall, and he and Horn stand back and consider it for a moment. The portrait, apparently, is one that Horn has commissioned for another A.T.&T. commercial.

Horn steps forward and then steps back again. "I don't know," he says. "Maybe it's the color. Maybe there's something funny about the color."

"I really worked hard on the color," the other man says.

"But the face just isn't right," says Steve. "It doesn't have a nice look."

"Sure, it has a nice look," says the man. "The problem is the hair. You said the hair should be long, but you didn't say how long."

"I'm not worried about the hair," says Steve. "The hair is all right. But I have problems with the face."

The man walks forward and picks up the painting. "You only called me two days ago, and I been working since then," he says.

"I need it the seventeenth," says Steve. "See what you can do. A nice look."

After the painter has departed, a few other details need to be attended to, and then, with the arrival of Gaston and Elliott, the group is ready to set out for the second day of shooting on "Tap Dancing." The white truck and two of the vans are already on their way to the day's location, which is in Scarsdale. The rest of the convoy, which consists of two other vans (one containing Palazzo and the talent and the other containing Vincent and the coffee and bagels and doughnuts, both vans being in continual walkie-talkie communication), follows Steve's station wagon, which is driven by Steve, with Linda Horn in the front seat and Gaston and Elliott in the back.

On the drive up into the country, Steve is in a good mood, despite the problems with the oil painting, because the New York Rangers won a key hockey game and so now have (he believes) a reasonable chance of winning the Stanley Cup. "They could do it," he says. "They're a good, young team. *Fast*. They could do it if they don't blow it in the clutch. I love hockey, but really I'm just a sports freak. I love to watch sports. It probably started when I was a kid growing up in Brooklyn. We had the Brooklyn Dodgers then. What heroes they were! In those days, you had a team—you had a *team*. You didn't have a bunch of free agents drifting around the country. I never did much sports myself as a kid—the usual sandlot stuff. I guess you could say I was kind of artistic, but the truth is in those days I knew more about what I didn't want to do than what I wanted to do. My dad was a pharmacist, and I knew I didn't want to become a pharmacist. I graduated from Pratt with a degree in advertising art. Then for a while I got very interested in serious art. I studied at night at Columbia: thirteenth- and fourteenth-century Italian painting. Really beautiful things! I thought I wanted to teach art, and I even took a teaching job, but I only taught a couple of classes—it wasn't for me. I was in advertising at the time—an art director—but I was also into photography. Still photography—a lot of artistic stuff—which is a hard way to make a living. So in the early sixties I started doing commercial photography—mostly stills. Later, it was a logical move to film. I definitely don't regret the time I spent doing the artistic stuff, though, because I'm always using some of that knowledge and technique in my present work."

Gaston asks Steve if he has ever thought of branching out in film beyond commercials.

"Actually, we've been giving a lot of thought to getting into movies," Steve says. "There are a lot of possibilities in movies."

"A lot of headaches, too," says Linda.

"Definitely a lot of headaches," says Steve. "That's why I'm not crazy to get into feature films. I mean, a guy could lose his shirt that way. But TV movies—I think that's different. Those are tight operations: no messing around, no fuss, a lot of structure. I think my kind of talent could work out well in TV movies. I mean, from time to time—something extra. I don't need the work, after all. I just haven't found the right script yet."

The shooting set this time is the Zacharia house. A fairly large white frame building, it is definitely newer than the Dambach house, in New Jersey, and also has a somewhat more sophisticated interior décor: glass tables, lacquered furniture, contemporary rugs, a plenitude of houseplants. Where the Dambach house might be described as traditional suburban and fairly prosperous, the Zacharia house is rather more elegantly suburban and slightly more prosperous. Outside are several acres of carefully landscaped lawn, including a couple of dogwood trees in fine pink bloom; also a swimming pool; also a handsome porch. Once again, though, Steve Horn and his crew, having gained at considerable effort and expense a locale of some particularity (as in the case of the Dambach

house's 1770-ness, which as a mise-en-scène seemed
scarcely visible behind the little tap-dancing group
around the baby-grand piano), now, with a brisk display of equipment-unloading industry and logistical
know-how, seem to be intent on transforming the
Zacharia *House & Garden* sun porch into a similar
studiolike setting. Thus, furniture is shifted to the
side or removed altogether; a picture is taken down,
as causing too much reflection; the modern carpet is
rolled up; some throw pillows, apparently brought
out that morning from New York, are arranged in a
manner thought appropriate. Meanwhile, the big
lights are being set up; the camera is hauled into
position; cables seem to run in all directions; and, in
a tactful, guestlike gesture of concern for the Zacharia
dark wood floors (which have the look of having been
spruced up by the absent host—as does the rest of the
house, even to fresh little guest towels in the downstairs bathroom—for the Horns' arrival), Alayne and
Ron Palazzo begin to cover them with sheets of coarse
white canvas.

The vignette that will be shot here today is the yoga
vignette. This consists of two scenes: a black girl and a
white girl, one with a cat, the other with a baby, each
girl upside down in a headstand, each talking on the
phone. The two actresses are present, in a side room,
where they are being made up and fitted with leotards.
The baby is here: a girl of about two. She is Vincent's
baby, and is accompanied by Vincent's young wife.
The cat is here: Mittens, a professional cat. There is

also a spare, or substitute, cat, Ophelia. Both of them are in a carrying box on the lawn, accompanied by their handler. Apparently, all that is needed before shooting can begin is the arrival of rain: not rain from the dull-gray sky above, which, in fact, is already beginning to scatter a thin, halfhearted film of drizzle, but rain from a rain machine that Steve Horn has ordered for the purpose of providing a suitable background effect on the windows of the sun porch while the white girl is performing her yoga headstand.

"You'd think they could just use the *regular* rain," says the white actress, whose name is Melodie, and who is standing in the middle of the floor in a bright-pink leotard.

"That's God's rain," says Vincent, who has recently removed his shirt but has left his hat on. "It doesn't show up on film. We need Billy's rain."

Fortunately, Billy and his rain machine soon arrive —a large, cheery young man driving a black pickup truck with lots of pipe in the back, and followed by an older, saturnine man driving a bright-orange tree-spraying truck, whose spraying tank is presumably full of water. Renewed activity now takes place, both inside and outside the house, and the walkie-talkies are once again put to use, by Vincent, who stands outside the sun-porch windows with Billy and his pipes, and receives instructions from Steve Horn on the inside, relayed by Ron Palazzo. Essentially, the rain equipment consists of several tall, rickety-looking T-shaped pipe systems set up on the grass and connected by a maze of hoses to the orange tank truck, in front of the house—with the "rain" supposed to emanate from the crossbar at the top of the T, this bar being laced with apertures, like a flute or, possibly, a very leaky pipe, which, of course, it is. Now the water is turned on, and what results is a drenching of the windows. In due course, the rain pipes are moved a few feet back— not an easy task, because the lawn is sloping. Again the water is turned on: another drenching, this time apparently on the wrong part of the windows. Outside, more shifting about of the cumbersome pipes.

Steve takes the walkie-talkie from Palazzo. "We want fine spray in the front," he says. "You're giving us coarse spray."

Soon there is another spray, similar to the one before.

Steve says: "Look, you guys, we want fine spray in the front and coarse spray in the back."

In response, the walkie-talkie in his hand emits a furious burst of static. Steve gives the machine to Palazzo and asks him to deliver the message in person to Vincent and Billy.

Now there are about a half-dozen men outside: two of them lugging one of the big 4-K lights into place beside a tree and then setting up one of the multicolored umbrellas to protect it from God's rain, which is beginning to fall a bit more persistently; two others with one of the ladders, which is now extended to its limit, some thirty feet, and placed with its base in a pond about two feet deep, and with its top rungs against a branch of a large elm nearby. Vincent stands knee-deep in the water and holds the ladder while one of the grips, Tommy Drohan, climbs to the branch with a length of rope and loops it over the branch; another large light is now brought out and tied to one end of the rope, and pulled up to the height of the tree branch.

Steve himself appears outside, wearing his baseball cap right way around. "That's good with the light," he says. "Can we get it any higher?"

"We can raise the tree," says Vincent.

"No—I mean, can we tighten the rope a few feet?"

"I don't think so," says Vincent.

"Sometimes I hate this rain stuff," says Steve. "When it works, it can be very nice, but the only way rain looks any good is if you light it properly." He starts to go back in. "Remember, the rain has to hit the windows, but not too much," he says.

After a few more tries, the rain equipment seems to be set, and, inside, Melodie is ready, and Steve is behind the camera, and the baby is waiting in the wings.

Steve says: "O.K., Melodie, let's try the headstand."

Melodie gets herself partway up, and then Alayne and Linda stabilize her on either side. "I'm O.K.," Melodie says, from upside down. Alayne and Linda leave her on her own.

"Very nice," says Gaston. "Is that a classic yoga position?"

"Yoga is pretty loose," says Ron Palazzo.

"She's looking good," says Steve.

"Just a minute, Steve," says Linda. "We've got a problem."

Steve and Linda walk over to one side of the room and have a private conference. The problem, it turns out, is that Melodie is not wearing a bra, and so her nipples are clearly in evidence through the pink leotard: perhaps not very noticeable but at least slightly noticeable. Melodie is asked to turn herself right side up. Gaston, Elliott, Steve, and Linda now confer.

Gaston says: "Why can't she just put on a bra?"

Linda says: "Because she didn't bring one."

Elliott says: "Maybe we can tape them."

Steve says: "Maybe they don't really show."

Linda says: "They show, all right."

Melodie and Linda now go off to a side room, where several attempts, all unsuccessful, are made to cover up the nipples with little crosses of adhesive tape. Kleenex is thought of, tried, and abandoned. Finally, Linda surrenders her own bra to Melodie, and both women reappear: Melodie, suitably protected, to resume her upside-down position; Linda, wearing over her silk blouse a loose sweater borrowed from the prop department, to stand between Steve and Gaston.

The scene with Melodie, the baby, and the rain takes most of the morning to complete. The action is supposed to go pretty much as follows: Melodie (having been stabilized in her upside-down position by Alayne and then left on her own) starts talking on the telephone (presumably to her friend in California, the pretty black girl), whereupon the baby (who has been brought just out of camera range by her mother and then gently propelled forward) toddles over toward Melodie and tries an imitation headstand of her own. What actually happens is that sometimes the baby toddles in and then toddles right out again, and sometimes she toddles in and doesn't do the little headstand, and sometimes she does the headstand but then suddenly walks out again. Once, after completing her headstand (which means mostly bending over with her head on the floor), the baby simply falls down.

"That's very cute," says Steve. "I want that again."

Numerous attempts are now made to have the baby fall down after her headstand, though on the few occasions that the baby—a stalwart little soul called Lily—complies with instructions the fall is usually in the wrong direction. By now, Melodie is fairly drenched in sweat, so after each take Joanna runs forward to dry her under her arms with a blow dryer, and Richard Hartenstein dabs at her face with some tissues.

Steve says: "*One* more time. This time, I want her to fall down."

Melodie says: "Who do you want to fall down?"

Steve says: "Not you—you just stay as you are, upside down. O.K.?"

They do it again, but the baby simply beams and wanders off.

Steve says: "*Damn,* I wish she'd fallen down then. Why won't she fall down?"

They do it again, but now the baby spins around and claps her hands.

"How about hand clapping?" says Gaston. "That's very cute."

"I agree it's cute, but it's not *really* cute, like falling down," says Steve. "O.K., one last time."

This time, the baby wanders listlessly toward upside-down Melodie and begins to cry.

Steve says: "No crying."

The baby is hauled off and briefly comforted, and then propelled forward again. This time, the toddle is fine, the headstand is fine, and the final fall is fine.

Steve says: "Absolutely perfect. Congratulate that baby."

Melodie tumbles to the floor.

"You're looking good," says Vincent. "Steve, shall we turn off the rain?"

"Turn off the rain," says Steve.

Lunch is dispensed on the back porch: a cafeteria arrangement of various salads, fruit, cheese, one hot chafing dish of beef Stroganoff, a chocolate cake—all of which have been brought out from the city by a catering service. During lunch, there is a new arrival: Ed DiBenedetto, a short, trim, fortyish man wearing blue-jeans and a safari jacket, who is an art director at N. W. Ayer and also a member of Jerry Pfiffner's Creative Group, and is the man who was responsible for the creation of the yoga vignette.

DiBenedetto says: "I think the yoga is a nice situation. It has a touch of the unique, if you ask me, but it's not way overboard. I mean, gals actually do this yoga stuff; they stand on their heads. You know, it's hard to remember later how a particular idea comes to you. I was in my office one day last winter when Jerry dropped by and said he needed a couple of situations. That was definitely the impetus. But why yoga? I don't have the foggiest idea about yoga myself. I think I was looking for something different, something novel—an unusual way of using the product. Unusual but also showing emotion. The thing about these phone ads is that what we're really doing is selling emotion. I mean, we're not inundated with selling the product, with having to sell the telephone as a piece of hardware. The way I see it, we have to sell the emotion that people bring to it, which, of course, is harder—it tests your skills."

After lunch, the crew sets up for the next scene—this time with the black girl, whose name is Leslie, and who wears a bright-yellow leotard. Everybody now moves to a room on the top floor of the house, and this means that the camera, the lights, the reflectors, the videotape equipment, the wires, the cables, the canvas sheets, and so forth, also move. Upstairs is what appears to be a children's room—perhaps a children's game room, for a miniature pool table, a doll house, and a television set are being pushed aside for a new arrangement. Someone carries in a wicker armchair, which has been brought out on the prop truck from New York.

Steve is lying on the floor, with his camera also on

the floor, and he and the camera remain there throughout the shooting. "I'm not sure about wicker," he says. "Do condominiums have wicker?"

"Sure they have wicker," says Gaston. "Some of them have wicker."

Steve says: "It doesn't seem to me wicker says condominium."

A compromise is reached with a chair from another room; also a modern-style standing lamp, which is approved of as having a condominium look. Also, the television set is brought back into camera range. But now there is a problem with Leslie's leotard. Ed DiBenedetto had expected blue—navy blue.

"The yellow just isn't right," he says. "I don't think I'm being too subjective."

Linda says: "We don't have any navy blue out here, but we have some yellow shorts."

DiBenedetto says: "I'm bothered by the yellow. It's too garish."

Steve says: "Maybe the shorts will be cute."

Leslie is dispatched to put on the shorts. Meanwhile, the woman (a middle-aged, motherly sort) who brought the cats is ushered into the room, clutching Mittens.

Steve says: "I don't want that cat running wild. Does she do what you tell her?"

The woman says: "Mittens is very well trained."

Now Leslie returns, indeed looking cute in yellow running shorts, and the shooting gets under way. First, Richard Hartenstein de-sweats her forehead. Then

Alayne and Linda help Leslie get upside down. Then Alayne and Joanna attempt to tape the telephone to the side of Leslie's head, since it is clear that she is nowhere as adept as Melodie at holding a headstand.

Steve says: "O.K., everyone. Cat lady, remember, when I say 'Cat,' put the cat down. O.K., let's go. Camera."

Leslie, upside down, is launched into her telephone spiel: "Oh, *really?* How are you? You're *kidding* me. Oh, *really?* You don't say."

Steve says: "Cat."

The cat lady, who is crouched about six feet from Leslie, out of camera range behind a door, now puts the cat down, but the cat goes nowhere—just stands there and looks at the cat lady. "Go on, Mittens," says the cat lady in a loud stage whisper.

Steve says: "Cut! O.K., cat lady, I thought you had a trained cat."

The cat lady says: "She's a wonderful cat, but sometimes she needs a little time."

Steve says: "Well, just tell me when you and she are ready."

The cat lady says: "I'm sure she's ready now. Aren't you, Mittens?"

They do it again. This time, the cat walks forward but goes behind Leslie.

Steve says: "Cat lady, that cat's got to walk across *in front.*"

The cat lady says: "Do you hear that, Mittens? *In front.*"

They do fifteen takes. Each time, there is a problem with the cat, much as there was with the baby. Sometimes the cat won't budge; sometimes it darts across in front of Leslie, or sometimes behind Leslie; on several occasions, when it has managed to do what it is supposed to and has returned to the cat lady out of camera range, the cat lady's arm or hand will suddenly appear from behind the door and become a part of the scene. Also, there is a growing problem with Leslie, whose cuteness is beginning to evaporate under the strain of holding herself upside down.

"This is getting a little *old*," she mutters at one point, having aborted the last take by collapsing in mid-scene.

"We're *all* getting a little old," says Steve, who is showing signs of grumpiness himself. "O.K., cat lady," he says. "We're going for broke next time."

The cat lady says: "Anything you say, Steve."

Steve says: "If I see that arm of yours in my lens, you'll never work in Scarsdale again."

The cat lady says: "We're going to try awfully hard."

They do the scene once more. It's nearly right. Again. It's nearly right, except that Mittens turns her behind to the camera.

"I'm really sorry, Steve," says the cat lady.

At last, they have it.

"O.K. Beautiful," says Steve. He gets up from the floor, stretches, removes his baseball cap, scratches his head. The crew has already started to move the equipment back down the stairs to the trucks. Steve walks down the stairs with Linda, followed by Gaston, Elliott, and Ed DiBenedetto.

DiBenedetto says: "I watched it on the video, and the cat reads very well."

Gaston says: "I think it had a very nice quality."

Steve says: "You know, sometimes those little human touches just about break your back."

Going Right to the Top

U P IN THE N. W. AYER OFFICES, HIGH ABOVE SIXTH
Avenue, Gaston Braun and Buzz Sawyer have been
conferring about phone booths. The problem to be re-
solved is in the Marine vignette, where the script calls
for the young recruit, newly shorn of hair, to be
phoning his father, who is a barber, back in the barbershop. The logical type of phone to be used would be
a phone-booth phone, for what other kind of phone
would a Marine recruit have at his disposal? But there
is a difficulty here, in that the Fort Tilden barracks,
where the vignette will be filmed, are no longer in use,
and no longer have phone booths on the premises. So
for a while this afternoon the two men have been
giving their time to a perusal of a large, plastic-covered
volume published—or, at least, issued—by the Western
Electric Company and titled *The Coin Telephone Enclosure Handbook*. "Coin telephone enclosure," apparently, is A.T.&T. parlance for "phone booth," a

venerable term that doubtless now has connotations rather too vulgar or casual to appeal to the readers for whom the volume is intended: the owners of small businesses in towns and shopping centers, whose prosperity and progressivism are clearly indicated in the *Handbook* by stylishly artistic renderings of gleaming drugstores, coffee shops, and motel restaurants, in the foreground of which stand equally gleaming and inviting examples of the company's current product line. Thus, an item that Gaston and Buzz have been lately studying is called the "Sentry Standard Enclosure": a fairly typical phone booth of recent design, which means that there is almost no booth to it at all, but instead a sort of glass shield has been stuck on around the top part of what used to be the booth, through which the enclosure-user can presumably see the trucks and buses that are making it impossible to hear what is being said to him, and whose sentrylike qualities will stand him in good stead in the event of a modest Boy Scout attack. The caption beneath the "Sentry Standard Enclosure" reads as follows: "A coin telephone is a welcome convenience to most people. When a phone is needed and it's in or just outside your premises, everybody benefits—especially you."

Gaston says: "I like the old booths better."

Buzz says: "I'm not sure we can get the old booths."

Gaston says: "A phone booth should *look* like a phone booth."

Buzz says: "I've been on the phone all day with

New York Telephone, and they say they don't have any left."

Gaston says: "What did they do with them all—ship them to South America, like the trolley cars?"

Buzz says: "They say they don't have any left to lend."

Gaston says: "The *phone* company?"

In due course, Gaston departs to make preparatory arrangements for several other A.T.&T. commercials, which he is also working on, leaving to Buzz the task of tracking down phone booths through the bureaucracy of the New York Telephone Company. First, he calls a man who handles only sales, and who switches him to another man, who also handles sales and promises delivery in four months, and who switches him to a woman, who says she doesn't have time for this sort of thing, and who switches him to another man, who says he knows just the person for Buzz to speak to, and gives him the name of someone with Pacific Telephone, in Los Angeles. Buzz calls Los Angeles, but the man is out.

Buzz Sawyer (his first name, which he never seems to use, is William) is in some ways too good to be true. One wonders, for example: Was the name designed to fit the man, or the man designed to fit the name? He is about six feet tall, with blond hair, blue eyes, what used to be called a frank, open countenance, and the air of cheerful invulnerability of an R.O.T.C. second lieutenant. Buzz is twenty-five years old, and in the hierarchy of A.T.&T. account people at N. W. Ayer he is somewhere between the top and the bottom, although perhaps not quite in the middle. At the top is George Eversman, a senior vice-president (like Jerry Pfiffner on the creative side) and management supervisor, the latter meaning that he is in charge of all client-servicing aspects of the Long Lines account. Below Eversman are three account supervisors—for residence, business, and international. The account supervisor for residence is Fred McClafferty. Below McClafferty are three account executives, Buzz himself being the senior account executive, with two account executives below him—one in charge of research and the other in charge of dealing with the operating companies of the Bell System. Buzz has been with the agency for a little over a year and a half. Before that, he worked for a television production company in Dallas. "I'm a guy who moved around a lot," he says.

Buzz Sawyer talks about his job: "My job is primarily to service the account, which means, for instance, to keep the lines of communication open between the client and our creative people. On this shoot, I'd say that one of my main functions has been to make sure that the equipment needs are properly met. You see, although the director, Steve Horn, is responsible for all the theatrical props, he isn't responsible for client props—for instance, the telephones, or even the little lights inside some of the telephones. These little lights burn out very rapidly the way Steve is using them—plugging them into standard power sources—and they have to be replaced. My function is to make sure that we have enough of them on hand and, of course, also have the right phone equipment on hand—Trimline, Touch Tone, even dial. Take the matter of the phone booths. I could probably pick up the phone right now and go right to the top of Long Lines headquarters, in Bedminster, New Jersey. But I don't want to—not unless I really have to. My aim is to handle the problem, and solve it, within the system."

Buzz Sawyer talks about the advantages of a diagnostic approach: "To begin with, the account branch is primarily service-oriented, and the creative branch is creative-oriented, so for a more diagnostic approach you have to go to our research people. What we ask them for is simple copy pre-testing, to find out if a piece of copy communicates. What we do there is we go out on location, but we don't take videotape or film —we do stills. With these stills, using them scene by scene, we produce a photomatic. That means you take the stills and you shoot them onto videotape—only you vary it a little with zoom and dissolves to get a little movement—and then the research people contract with an outside supplier to test the photomatic against a target audience. Often, we use a regular UHF channel in Philadelphia, with a regular audience. In other words, the UHF station will be showing *Gilligan's Island* at four on a certain afternoon with eight commercial spots, so we buy one spot for our photomatic, and then, the day before the show, the research people call around to members of the public and say,

'Please watch this program; we're going to ask you some questions later,' and then after the show they call back and say, 'Did you remember any of the commercials?' If they actually remember your commercial, that's unaided recall, which is the most valuable. Most of the time, though, you have to do a little prodding— for instance, 'Did you remember the phone-company commercial?'—which is called aided recall and is generally less diagnostic. The result is that, for the purpose of being more diagnostic, we've been employing a more tactical research approach. This is our van operation. We move a van into a shopping center. First, you go into the shopping center and try to get people out of the shopping center into the van. That way, you get a reaction profile. And after screening the photomatic you ask diagnostic questions. For example, you might ask the viewer 'Was the commercial humorous?' and then right away you ask him to grade the humorous quotient on a scale of zero to five."

At four in the afternoon, the man from Pacific Telephone calls back. It turns out it's true that he has phone booths at his disposal—phone booths that can be rented virtually free for a commercial shoot. Indeed, the man's job with Pacific Telephone is to provide phone booths as props in movies and television programs.

"That's terrific," says Buzz. "Can you ship two standard booths here? You know, the old-fashioned kind with doors. . . . That's what I said: Can you ship two phone booths to New York?"

There is a pause.

"I see," says Buzz. "I see your point."

After he puts the phone down, he calls Gaston, on the floor above. "Gaston, this is Buzz," he says. "You know, I may have to go all the way to the top for those phone booths after all."

Medium Teeth

ODAY IS A REAL MESS OF A DAY: A REAL SPRING downpour; no fooling around with halfhearted drizzle or with rain machines. The film crew is out in Englewood, New Jersey, shooting the toothless-kid vignette for "Tap Dancing," but, fortunately, once again inside: this time, inside the Mettler house, a pleasantly suburban house that seems to possess intrinsically no style at all; that is, neither a noticeably old-fashioned aura nor contemporary chic. Perhaps modern-American-family style is what it is, or has, and, as if to lend strength to this theory, wherever the members of the film crew trudge or wander, in and out of the cozy little rooms, carrying their great lights and assorted electrical bric-a-brac, one or another of them is forever stumbling over a toy or a discarded boot or a pet or a tennis racquet. Mrs. Mettler herself is on hand: an amiable, businesslike woman, who, with Ray Guarino, the location scout, is trying to set up a table in the basement recreation room for the film crew's usual midmorning-snack fiesta of coffee, bagels, soft drinks, and little pineapple-and-ham canapés.

Mrs. Mettler observes Vincent Donohue coming in from the rain-soaked driveway, wearing his usual costume of hat, cigarette, and undershirt, with—clearly for the occasion—sporty white trousers.

"That young man is going to get awfully wet," says Mrs. Mettler.

"He'll be O.K.," says Ray.

"I have some raincoats," says Mrs. Mettler.

"I'm sure he brought his own raincoat," says Ray.

Ray introduces Mrs. Mettler to Elliott Manketo as he arrives. "Mrs. Mettler is a force in our business," Ray explains. "She has one of the biggest location lists in the area."

"It all started with Steve Horn and Tonka Toys, years ago," says Mrs. Mettler. "One of Steve's people was looking for a porch that would be just right for a toy commercial, and he drove right down *this* street and saw *this* porch—the one outside in the back as you come in. Afterward, I thought I'd call around to my friends to see if they didn't want to show off their houses, too, and then friends called other friends, and pretty soon I was in business with my list."

"I imagine I've seen your house a lot on television," says Elliott.

"You might have seen it in a Johnson & Johnson a little while ago," says Mrs. Mettler. "Though just the upstairs bedroom."

Down the stairway comes a blast of vaguely familiar music—the "Tap Dancing" theme song, "Reach Out," or, rather, a version of it—which is rapidly hushed down.

"Those are my guys," says Elliott, excusing himself and heading up the stairs.

"It's a pleasure!" calls Mrs. Mettler.

On the second floor, in a child's small room—presumably a girl's room, since it contains a doll house, a canopied bed, and frilly pillows, along with a poster of Peter Frampton—Jerry Pfiffner and Gaston Braun, now joined by Elliott, are gathered around a child-sized desk listening to the playback of a tape recorder.

First, some bouncy piano chords, played as if on an upright in an empty studio. Then a man's voice—pleasant, somewhat on the high side, not altogether trained—singing to piano accompaniment:

> Your audience is ready,
> So put on your dancin' shoes.
> Reach out and touch someone.
> They'll love it if ya do.
>
> Reach out,
> Reach out and touch someone.
> Reach out,
> Call up and share your day.
>
> It's always great fun
> Finding out who won
> And sharing a winning smile.
> Reach out,
> Call up and share a smile.

Jerry says: "I think it's too slow."

Gaston says: "Well, it's a ballad."

Jerry says: "Even if it's a ballad, it's too slow. Did you time it?"

Gaston consults his stopwatch and says: "It comes in at twenty-five."

Jerry says: "You know, you could probably just speed it up in the front and then put in another line at the end."

They play the song once again on the tape machine. Then again, and again.

Jerry says: "It should be faster."

Gaston says: "It's a funny thing—normally I like ballads."

Elliott says: "Remember, we're going to have all those cuts. Zip. Zip. Zip."

Jerry says: "What can we take from the front?"

Gaston says: "Well, the time comes in at thirteen down to the first 'Reach out.' "

Jerry says: "We ought to be able to do quite a lot with thirteen seconds."

Meanwhile, in another bedroom on that floor, the crew, under Steve Horn's supervision, is preparing the set for the toothless-kid vignette, which calls for a young (toothless) boy and his mother to be watching a television set while the boy's father (a yet-to-be-signed toothless hockey player) is supposedly on camera in the locker room after a victorious game. The problems here have been minor, though scarcely nonexistent. First, the bed was in the wrong place and had

113

to be moved, and this meant that much of the furniture in the room had to be rearranged or taken out. Then the bedspread was the wrong color, and so was taken off. This left the sheets and pillowcases, which were also wrong (their colors were "too busy"), and so were removed, while Linda and Alayne went to find new sheets and pillowcases and remake the bed. Then, there was the matter of the television set—for apparently when one wants to show on film the special glow-and-flicker of a television set in a room without showing the actual image on the television screen one cannot simply turn the TV set on and film the room, because the glow-and-flicker won't show up in the negative. As Steve explains it, "You get the glow if you're lucky, but you never get the flicker." So he put together a simulated-flicker device: a rod about three feet long from which dangle strips of blue plastic ribbon. A crew member sits out of camera range, holds the rod with its ribbons in front of the TV set, and jiggles the rod and the ribbons (with a light playing on them), thus creating both glow and flicker. But now the rod is missing.

"Vincent, I don't believe it," Steve says.

"It may be in the food truck," Vincent says.

"Would you please check the food truck?" says Steve.

In the corridor outside the film-set bedroom, Kenneth Saluk, age six, is waiting, wearing a prop-department bathrobe, carrying a coloring book, and accompanied by his mother, Adrienne Saluk; a few feet behind Mrs. Saluk stands Mary-Jane Foster, also in a bathrobe, who will play Kenneth's mother in the vignette.

"Kenny, don't you want to color?" says Mrs. Saluk.

"I already colored," says Kenneth, who is stocky and sandy-haired.

"Kenny is definitely in demand for this type of role," says Mrs. Saluk, "because, of course, he's missing his front teeth. He had them extracted when he was two and a half, because he fell from a bike, and the dentist said they should come out. I have four boys in all, and three of them have tried out for commercials. Actually, my twins were selected three or four times to do a national commercial, and I think they did really well, but each time the commercial never actually got off the ground—I don't know why. You take the bad luck with the good, I always say. But I definitely encourage them to do the work, because it's a good way to build a nest egg for college. In Kenny's case, he's in demand now because of his missing teeth, and that's been very nice; only last month, he was doing a big commercial for Sunbeam bread—four different locations, including Staten Island. The tag line was when the mommy says 'The bread is so delicious he even eats the crust!' and then Kenny puts the crust in his mouth and gives a big smile, so the missing teeth show. Very cute. The agency people were real pleased. But they said it was going to be shown network and it was only shown somewhere in Pennsylvania and somewhere in North Carolina and someplace out West—definitely not in New York. It's hard for Kenny when they don't show it locally, because if people can't *see* you on TV they don't believe you were ever on. Some months, I take Kenny into the city on casting calls about three or four times a week. I'm telling you, it isn't easy from where we live, on Long Island. But, frankly, I'm looking for Kenny to expand the variety of his roles. I mean, right now he doesn't really get many across-the-board calls, on account of he's a specialty. Of course, he's definitely at an advantage on the toothless calls. I have to say that he's done very well with that type of call. But the trouble is, those are his baby teeth that are missing, and so when the new teeth grow in he'll have to compete across the board."

Down the hall, in the little girl's bedroom, Jerry and Gaston continue to struggle with the music and lyrics for "Tap Dancing"—or, rather, the suggested music, which was composed the day before by David Lucas to words by a free-lance lyricist named Don Wood, and put on what is called a scratch track, for use in shooting and cutting the film. Elliott has left to check the videotape equipment, with its TV relay downstairs, while Gaston and Jerry play and replay the little song.

Gaston says: "I wonder if it's really a question of shorter or maybe a question of rhythm."

Jerry says: "It's a question of shorter *and* rhythm."

116

Jerry is sitting on a child's chair, with a notebook and pencil in hand, making notes about the length and timing of individual lines. "I don't see that we can wait for those stretch-out chords to end."

Gaston says: "It seems to me what we need is tempo. More tempo."

Jerry says: "Definitely something faster up front. Something we can cut to. Now, suppose we take the 'Reach out and touch someone, they'll love it if ya do' and pair that with the yoga? Then we can have four lines of lyric before we go to the hockey."

Elliott returns to announce that shooting is about to begin.

Gaston says: "I like the concept, but does it work structurewise? I mean, having the hockey as a sendoff?"

Jerry says: "Structurewise, it works fine. We take the instant of the hockey player smiling . . ."

Gaston says: "And *extend* his smile . . ."

Jerry says: "And *key* to the lyric 'Share a smile.' It's perfect."

Back in the other bedroom, Steve Horn is crouched behind his camera, and various members of his crew are crowded in with him: Linda is standing beside him; Alayne Baxter is against one wall, behind a large light; Vincent and Loet Farkas are against the opposite wall, beside another large light; Ron Palazzo is next to Vincent; Tommy Drohan is on the floor beside the TV set, holding the just-found plastic-ribbon device; Ray is in the doorway, where he is now joined by

Gaston, Jerry, and Mrs. Mettler; and on the bed, half sitting and half reclining in a son-and-mother pose, are Kenny Saluk and Mary-Jane Foster.

Jerry says: "I wonder if it wouldn't be more interesting to have the kid sitting on the floor."

Steve says: "O.K., kid, try sitting on the floor right in front of the TV set."

Kenny Saluk sits cross-legged on the floor.

Jerry says: "I'm not sure that's interesting enough."

Steve says: "Kenny, back on the bed. Let's see your smile."

Kenny goes back and sits on the bed and smiles his gap-toothed smile.

Steve says: "That's nice, Kenny."

Jerry says: "I'm looking for something that's a bit more *interesting*—that isn't just another mom and kid on a bed."

Linda says: "What about he takes off his sneakers?"

Jerry says: "But not too much of a cuddly thing."

Steve says: "Look, the mom isn't the important thing. The important thing is the teeth. Kid, try sitting more to the right."

Jerry says: "I like that."

Linda says: "The mom seems low to me."

Jerry says: "The mom is incidental."

After Kenny and Mary-Jane have been positioned a few more times, Steve does a few takes, but something still seems to be wrong.

Jerry says: "I'm not getting that special feeling."

Steve says: "I know what you mean. How about we put dungarees on the kid?"

Gaston says: "Pajamas. The scene says pajamas."

Steve says: "Pajamas."

Kenny is sent off to be reequipped with pajamas. Meanwhile, Alayne and Linda get the bed back together, and Richard Hartenstein dabs at Mary-Jane's face with a handful of tissues. Kenny returns, with pajamas on under his robe, and he and Mary-Jane resume their positions on the bed, and the shooting continues.

After four more takes, Steve says: "I'm pleased, but I'm not excited."

Jerry says: "I think I have a brainstorm. How about a peanut-butter sandwich?"

Steve says: "That's very good."

Linda says: "I don't know if we have peanut butter."

Jerry says: "Peanut butter would be best."

This time, Alayne is dispatched downstairs to rustle up a peanut-butter sandwich. Meanwhile, Steve banters with Kenny.

"How are you doin', Kenny?" Steve says.

"Good," says Kenny.

"*Real* good?" says Steve.

"Real good," says Kenny.

Alayne returns with a peanut-butter sandwich on a plate, which she puts on the bed next to Kenny, and a glass of milk, which she puts on top of the TV set.

Gaston says: "We can't have the milk there."

Steve says: "It looks good. A nice quality."

Gaston says: "I know, but then the phone company gets letters saying, 'How could you leave that milk there? The kid is going to spill the milk on the set, and the house will go up in sparks, and all those people will be burned to death.' "

Steve says: "They'd say all that?"

Gaston says: "All that."

Linda takes the milk away, and Steve does a few more takes.

Jerry says: "The sandwich adds, but there's something lacking."

Steve says: "He's watching the end of the game, isn't he? So the sandwich should be eaten."

Gaston says: "Not *all* eaten. Then there'd be no sandwich."

Steve says: "A couple of bites. It's more real that way. Alayne, take a couple of bites out of the sandwich."

Gaston says: "Not large bites."

After Alayne has discreetly bitten into the sandwich, Steve continues. "O.K., Kenny," he says, from behind the camera. "Get ready, get ready, now hold your chin up, ready, lights, camera, now get the phone up, not too far, don't hide the mouth."

On the bed, meanwhile, Mary-Jane and Kenny are improvising the dialogue, with Mary-Jane saying, "Say '*Hi*, Daddy.' Daddy just won the big game. Say how you're so *glad* he won," and with Kenny beaming and saying "Hi, Daddy, I'm glad you won, I'm glad you won."

Steve says: "We're close. We're getting close."

Jerry comes up from checking the TV monitor.

"I like the wave of the hand," he says.

Steve says: "The wave is very good. But I'm seeing teeth the whole time. Do we want that much teeth?"

Jerry says: "Medium teeth."

Once more, they do the scene. "Let's do it, Kenny," says Steve. "Chin up. Wave. Wave that arm. Laugh. You gotta laugh, Kenny. Keep that phone away from the mouth. Yes, show the teeth."

It's over.

"I think that one was really beautiful," Steve says. "How long does it run?"

Jerry says: "I'd say anywhere between two and three seconds."

Gaston says: "It's well into three seconds."

Outside in the corridor, Mrs. Mettler and Mrs. Saluk are discussing children. "The important thing is not to apply too much pressure," says Mrs. Saluk. "So when Kenny says he doesn't want to do a job we don't do it. We just stay home. We don't worry about it. We don't pressure. We just stay home."

Mary-Jane Foster is on the landing, having her makeup removed and then taking off the bathrobe, which has been covering a shirt and bluejeans. "I'm originally a Denver girl who came to New York to be a serious actress," she says. "I did a George Kaufman play Off Off Broadway a couple of years ago, and I've done a play at the Manhattan Theatre Club, but mostly I do commercials. Last year, I had a really terrific year, because I lucked into a Johnson & Johnson ad that played in ninety cities and brought in about fourteen thousand dollars, which is very unusual. I know that a lot of so-called serious actors look down on commercial work, but I think that's because they have a limited perspective. I'm proud of what I do, and I think it's refined my craft tremendously. Mainly, it's tightened my technique, and it's taught me how to cut out extraneous stuff. I mean, it's a very demanding form, because you've got only thirty seconds in which to establish a character, so you don't have time for all that extraneous stuff around the edges. Of course, I'm lucky in that I have a regular, Midwestern, kind of all-American face, so I've been getting lots of jobs. But I won't do everything. I won't do those brutal pesticides that poison the environment, and I won't do douches. I mean, as you work your way up in the profession, you begin to set certain standards for yourself. In my case, you might say that my standards are basically political."

The Detached Communicator

Fred McClafferty is an N. W. Ayer veteran, having been with the agency for the past twenty-three years. He started in the media branch as a time buyer for radio and television, switched to account-executive work six years ago, and is now one of the three account supervisors on the A.T.&T. Long Lines account. He is in his late forties, trim, well dressed (today in a summer-weight gray suit), of medium height, with thin sandy hair, blue eyes, a generally youthful face, and a demeanor that is friendly and accommodating and, at the same time, altogether sure of itself.

Fred McClafferty talks about the need for a role model: "Well, from the very start—meaning more than a year ago, when the A.T.&T. agency task force began trying to work out a central direction for the campaign —our primary objective, you might say, was to devise a strategy that would give us a unified face. By this I mean that in the past Long Lines would often be saying one kind of thing in its advertising and the operating companies would be saying another kind of thing, usually focussing on rates, so you had the problem of company advertising coming from two different directions. So one of the first steps we had to take was to figure out a role model for what we were hoping to accomplish, and I'll frankly admit that our role model was McDonald's. I realize that some people might not think that McDonald's and the phone company have the same problems, or the same sort of problems, but the fact is that McDonald's has a national program and a national image, and it also has local situations handled by local agencies, and yet it's been enormously successful in developing a centralized theme. I mean, in one part of the country they may be advertising Egg McMuffins, and in another part of the country they may be advertising plastic cups, but no matter where you are you know that it's McDonald's advertising, and that's the truly important thing."

Fred McClafferty talks about the detached communicator. "Now, let me try to get into the heavy-to-medium-user philosophy for a moment. Basically, what this means is that we are targeting people who are already disposed toward making a long-distance phone call, who have already experienced making a long-distance phone call. But, frankly, we have in this country a very sizable body of *non-users*. The latest figures show, I think, that around forty per cent of the people in the country *just don't make long-distance phone calls*. Our first assumption, rather naturally, was that the reason all these people hadn't called out of town was that they were afraid of the cost—or had an outdated idea of what the cost might be. So we went into a number of specific areas in the country and we targeted a series of localized rate-information ads to this problem. What we found first was that there was a definite, though very moderate, increase in long-distance calling as a result of our advertising. But what we also found was that there remained a considerable number of people—whose profiles, incomewise and educationwise, sometimes indicated even a high-user category—who simply did not call long-distance. So the company did some psychographic-segmentation studies on these people, and what they discovered was that there are a number of people in the country who just don't have any relatives or friends, and, much more significantly, that there are an even greater number of people in the country who do have relatives and friends in other towns and states but who apparently just don't want to talk to them. In other words, these are people who actually possess cousins, uncles, old Army buddies, old college roommates, and so forth but just don't much care to speak to them, at least on the phone. The company has a name for this type of person: the detached communicator. We can beam commercials all year long at these people, and tell them about our terrific rates, and get them humming our theme song, but we can't get them to *care* about their friends enough to call them. Of course, our hope is that eventually this type of person will experience a change of psychology and become a normal communicator, but for the time being it really just isn't worthwhile to try to include them, targetwise, in our advertising."

Fred McClafferty discusses the element of guilt in phone-company advertising: "I suppose there's a small element of guilt in some of our advertising, but we try to keep it pretty light. In fact, we prefer to think of it in terms of obligation. What we have to remember is that the phone company is a regulated monopoly, a very large regulated monopoly, and so from a common-sense or public-relations standpoint it's not in the position of being able to beat consumers over the head, the way some companies do. In other words, there has to be a sort of subtle, good-taste kind of thing. You can suggest in an artistic manner that a person might feel better for making a phone call to a faraway friend, but it wouldn't be right to suggest that something terrible will happen to the person if they don't make the call —that they'll lose the girl or the boy and ruin their life. So what we try to do is keep the obligation level very light, and, of course, artistic, and relate it to an upbeat, positive theme. I think this was especially true in the way the creative people handled the third target response that was set by the task force. This was the concept of mutual reward—meaning that a long-distance phone call should be rewarding both to the person called *and* to the person who makes the call. I think this was something of a stride forward in our philosophy, because up to then our advertising had generally implied that the reward factor was obtained mainly by the person called. You should call your mother because *she'll* feel good. What we hadn't really considered until the task force called our attention to it was that by calling your mother *you'll* feel good also. So, armed with this knowledge of mutual reward, we've been able to introduce an element of obligation into our new campaign, but with a definitely positive side to it: *you* gain and *she* gains. I think it's one of the reasons our commercials have such a happy tone to them."

Billy Longo Gets Upgraded

I<small>T'S CLOSE TO NOON, AND ON</small> F<small>IRST</small> A<small>VENUE BETWEEN</small> Seventy-seventh and Seventy-eighth Streets six men are standing in a group on the sidewalk outside the Alfred Barber Shop, which, as barbershops in the city go, clearly belongs to a bygone era, though its ambience is not so much that of the elegant "tonsorial parlor" (now relentlessly resurrected in all the new shopping arcades) as of the classic, workaday, heterosexual, proletarian haircut. In fact, the place is somewhat shambling, and is unrelieved by either charm or camp: one long, narrow room which is decorated mainly with those little white tiles that are found in the cheaper Chinese restaurants or in airport washrooms. It contains four barber chairs; a sign that advertises "Regular Haircut $4, Hair Tonic 50¢, Long Hair $9"; an array of Brylcreem and Kreml bottles on a counter; and, today, a number of large and glowing lights, a movie camera mounted on a small dolly, and a great many people, two of whom are wearing white barber smocks and are being positioned around one of the chairs by Steve Horn.

Out on the sidewalk, the six men—one of whom is Alfred himself, four of whom are Alfred's barbers, wearing their civilian suits, and one of whom is an extra for today's shooting called Billy Longo—munch bagels from the back of Ron Palazzo's truck and peer in at the proceedings.

"It isn't the first time we been in an ad," says Alfred, who still speaks with a thick Italian accent, though he has owned and operated his little barbershop for twenty-five years. "Once before, we had the ad people. Headaches."

"They really take over a place, don't they?" says Billy Longo, who is fortyish, short, and chunky, somewhat resembles a hardboiled version of the comedian Tim Conway, and is wearing a sort of "Our Gang" newsboy's cap on his head.

"I mean they were *doin'* headaches," says Alfred. "Bufferin, you know what I mean? They have this guy gettin' a haircut. Right in there. Chair No. 3. The guy says, 'Ooh, I have a headache.' " Alfred claps his hand to his brow in anguish. "The barber guy, he says, 'You gotta use Bufferin for your bad head.' Maybe you seen the ad?"

"Nah, I didn't see it," says Billy Longo. "I work too hard to watch TV."

"You're an actor," says Alfred. "You have the glamorous life."

"Actin' is my first love," says Billy Longo, "but mainly I'm a building super. You know, a superintendent. I been a super for fourteen years, up in the Bronx. A very fine building. Sixty tenants. Before that, I drove a cab. Before that, I done all kind of jobs. Now I'm a family man, I got three boys in Catholic school, and I need the money. To be honest, I never trained as an actor, if you know what I mean, but I used to kid around a lot, and one day this guy said to me, 'You oughta make some money doin' this, you oughta go on the stage.' So I hustled my ass around to agents—boy, did I hafta hustle—and sooner or later I started getting jobs. I did a Miller Lite with Eddie Egan—I was the bartender. I did Allen Carpets. I did Paine Webber. I was even on the stage once. I was Henry Winkler's father in *42 Seconds from Broadway*. But let me tell you what happened with Paine Webber. I never went into the shoot with the intention of being an actor—a principal. I went in with the intention of being an extra. But what happened was that Steve Horn was directing that day and he upgraded me —right on the spot! He said I had the right look for the part. He's a terrific guy, one of the absolutely top directors; he knows what he wants, and he just goes and gets it. What I did in the Paine Webber was carry a TV set. We did thirty-three takes, but it wasn't too heavy. If I'd done it as an extra, I woulda made one hundred and seventy bucks for the day, no residuals. But since I was upgraded to principal, I got five thousand three hundred bucks so far. It's payin' for my sons' tuition, bless their hearts, and I even got something left over so I can take the wife out to dinner."

Inside the barbershop, Steve Horn seems to be experiencing some sort of difficulty, either with the barber chair or with the two actors, for first he moves them to one chair and then he moves them to another chair and then he takes the actor who has been playing the customer (a lean, gray-haired, rather distinguished-looking man) and makes him the barber, and puts the barber in the customer's chair.

"That guy's no barber," says Alfred.

"Don't worry Steve Horn knows what he's doing," says Billy Longo. "I'll tell you another thing. A lot of the actors are too much the prima donnas. They don't want to be extras. They want only to be the great actor. Me, I'm not looking to become a star. I mean, I'm a family man, I have my building, what do I want with being a star? But I'll tell you my philosophy. First, you don't hafta be a star if you're in the ballgame—the main thing is being in the ballgame. Secondly, there's always a chance you'll get upgraded. So I'm a happy man, I'm not stuck up, I'm not aimin' at the top, but I've done good work all the same. I think my best work was in the Shorehaven ad. That's some fancy club, one of the very fanciest—I've never seen such facilities. What I did was come out of the water, wearing a frogman suit—I mean, come right out of the sea and up the beach while the voice-over says, 'People will do *anything* to get into Shorehaven.' Everybody had a ball doing that ad; a lot of people told me they'll never forget it."

Just then, Steve Horn comes out onto the sidewalk, holding his baseball cap and scratching his head. He sees Billy Longo. "Billy Longo, come here," he says.

"Yes, sir," says Billy Longo.

"Billy, take off your cap," says Steve.

Billy takes off his cap, revealing a squarish, preponderantly bald head with a fringe of hair around the sides, somewhat like a monk's.

"Jesus, that's perfect," says Steve. "That's the look I want. Billy, go take one of those smocks and sit in the barber chair."

Billy starts for the barbershop, then pauses. "Steve, you upgradin' me?"

"I'm upgrading you, Billy," says Steve. "Only, don't talk so much." He puts the baseball cap back on his head and follows Billy through the doorway.

All You Have to Do Is
Work for It

"I'M TELLING YOU, WE'VE HAD HEADLINERS HERE," THE stage manager of the Beacon Theatre is saying to Loet Farkas, who is standing by watching Steve Horn's camera equipment being set up near one of the wings. "Some of the biggest names in the business have played the Beacon." He brings his mouth close to Farkas's ear in an approximation of a conspiratorial whisper. "Mind you, I'm talking about the *national* stage, the *American* stage, not some of these foreign circus acts you see nowadays." About a dozen feet away, seemingly unmindful of the stage manager, stand three Asians, clearly not members of the American national stage, inspecting the rope-and-pulley system, presumably on behalf of a troupe of Korean folksingers that will occupy the Beacon the following weekend.

"Didn't you know? We're a very international group," says Farkas, who himself is Dutch, and who is now trying to adjust the height of his camera.

"They said you was working for the phone company," says the stage manager.

"We're all Dutch," says Farkas.

"When I said foreign, I didn't mean Dutch," says the stage manager. "Half New York is Dutch. Did you know that?"

"See this camera?" says Farkas, stepping back from it for a moment. "This lens here is French: an Angenoux 20-120. The camera itself is German: an Arriflex. This here we call a door: it's Italian, a Cosmovision; in fact, we call it a Fellini door, because they made it specially for Fellini. Over here, the electrical system is from California, U.S.A. And right here, where you got this little TV camera built into the side, it's Dutch."

"Whaddaya know about that," says the stage manager.

"You could pick the whole system up for thirty-five thousand," says Farkas, "but it'd hafta be special order."

The Beacon Theatre, a large, old theater in the West Seventies, has row after row of red seats, an ample balcony (also red seats), rococo boxes with slightly peeling paint, and plaster statuary in the Grecian manner jutting out from niches along the walls. It looks like a classic Broadway musical-comedy theater of the nineteen-twenties which doesn't seem run-down so much as it seems to have somehow slipped its moorings and drifted uptown, where nobody has quite known what to do with it. Today, however, it seems to be returning, albeit briefly, to its former glory, for

134

once again there are bright lights on the stage, and a haze of smoke emanates from the orchestra seats (though there is no audience except a couple of mystified Koreans, and the smoke billows from smoke pots), and now a dozen musical-comedy chorus girls come on from the wings, wearing pink, leggy (though basically respectable) costumes, and, finally, there appears a splendidly old-fashioned figure of an entertainer in top hat and tails.

The chorus girls are all extras—chosen either with no subtlety at all or with great subtlety, for they range from long-legged homeliness to Rockette radiance, and as they teeter and thump about on the stage, practicing some elementary dance steps, it is clear that almost none of them were selected for intrinsic dancing ability.

Linda Horn watches them from the wings, where Steve is fiddling with the camera. "I love to watch dancers," she says. "Even not very good dancers. It's such hard work, and they want to succeed so badly. You know, I was a dancer. I started dancing when I was eight, and when I was thirteen I was in the American Ballet Theatre School, and a few years later I appeared on some programs with the American Ballet Theatre. It's difficult not to love dancing when you're close to such great talent. I was never great, of course, but I was pretty good—at least, for a while. I used to try awfully hard. Later, of course, other things come up in your life, though I kept close to dancing for a long while. I did some summer stock. I was lead dancer for a sea-son in the Westchester Ballet. I even taught dancing for a while at a school for wayward girls. But other things come up in your life. For example, my first marriage broke up, and I had three children to take care of. So I went to work for a commercial photographer, and that somehow led to Avon Products, and that somehow led to being editor of *Vogue Patterns* magazine, and that's how I met Steve."

"You were better than pretty good," says Steve.

"You never saw me," says Linda.

"No, but I can tell," says Steve.

Just then, Paul Reed, the actor playing the old entertainer, comes over, holding his top hat and simultaneously trying to tug on a pair of white gloves. Reed himself is a veteran actor, with a pink face, thin white hair, and a genial manner. He has appeared in a lifetime of plays and movies, mostly in supporting or character roles—though he was a principal in the 1968 musical *Promises, Promises*, and perhaps remains best known for his role in the popular TV series *Car 54, Where Are You?*

"How much fancy dancin' do you want me to do?" Reed asks Steve.

"The deal is this," says Steve. "You stand right over here, in front of the camera. Your back is to the stage, where a chorus number is still going on. You've just come off, after your world-famous tap-dancing routine, and you're getting a call from your granddaughter, who's gonna be a tap dancer in a school play. So you're gabbin' to her on the phone and you're still tappin' with your feet."

"Sounds good," says Paul Reed.

"Can we get him a cane?" says Jerry, who has just arrived with Gaston.

"We've got a cane somewhere," says Steve.

"Hi, Mr. Reed," says one of the leggy extras. "I saw you in *Car 54* when I was a kid. It was a really funny show. You were terrific."

"Thank you," says Paul Reed. "I bet you've certainly grown since then."

"I guess I have," says the girl.

Steve takes Linda aside. "Those dancers don't have to be Liza Minnellis," he says, "but they got to look like they can dance."

"You want me to rehearse them?" Linda says.

"Nothing too complicated," Steve says.

"Don't worry," says Linda.

Gaston is talking with Paul Reed, who has taken his place near what is supposed to represent a backstage prompting table, with a red phone on it.

"Have you danced in many musical shows, Mr. Reed?" Gaston asks.

"Not a one," says Paul Reed.

"In the movies?" says Gaston.

"Never," says Reed.

"I figured you must have been a young hoofer," says Gaston.

"I was never a young hoofer," says Paul Reed. "Fact

is, I never danced onstage before today. But I figure you guys'll put the taps in on the track and I'll have some fun. Hell, I'm seventy years old. Last year, I did Pillsbury and Kodak. Hell, I'm still having fun."

Steve Horn calls: "Are we ready? Vincent, not too much smoke!"

In the center of the stage, the chorus girls are lined up in two rows, arms extended to the sides, hands touching shoulders, hips and behinds swiveling to the left, to the right, to the left, to the right.

Linda Horn, half-shrouded in smoke, stands in front of them. "Come on, girls. One-two-three . . . one-two-three . . ."

One of the girls stumbles and nearly pulls down her line. "Maybe it should be either faster or slower," she says.

"It should be the way I'm doing it," says Linda. "O.K., now, one-two-three . . . one-two-three . . . four-five-six . . . four-five-six . . ."

"I think it's beginning to come together," says another of the girls.

"Of course it's coming together," says Linda. "All you have to do is work for it."

"Are we ready yet?" Steve Horn calls from behind the camera.

"We're getting there," says Linda.

You Don't Say "Stop!"

in the Army

HERE WE HAVE A STRANGE, BRIGHT DAY, WITH THE sun unusually luminous, even glowing, in a pale-blue sky, and with a brisk wind—nay, a high wind—blowing the scrawny trees, blowing the dusty bushes, blowing the tall dune grass on the horizon. Here, too, is an unlikely place, an unexpected cranny in the hitherto known world: the Queens seacoast. One might be tempted to say seashore, but there is no *plage* visible, or any sense of *plage*—only wild grasses, blackish rocks, and, in the distance, large outcroppings, seemingly of concrete, and, behind all that, the flat, gray-blue sea.

This, of course, is the background. The foreground is more banal and, as it were, plainspoken, though not without a certain romance in its austerity. We are referring now to Fort Tilden, a deserted Army base if there ever was one. Could these drab and empty old-style barracks ever have been occupied by rowdy non-coms, quivering recruits, haughty clerk-typists, bellicose master sergeants, and the like? On a nearby plot of scruffy grass (perhaps the former battalion parade ground?) , a lone figure, dressed half in jeans and half in a fatigue jacket—possibly in the fashion of the New Army, though with the bearing and demeanor of a lackadaisical convict—perambulates a lawnmower in vague ellipses, cutting dandelions and not much else. A flagpole remains in the center of a small rotunda of white-painted stones, but it is flagless: a symbol bereft of symbolism. In fact, the over-all effect is one not so much of desolation as of sudden deprivation of function: the stage set, for instance, of a science-fiction movie in which a mysterious nerve gas from outer space has killed off all the gallant, unsuspecting soldiers in their sleep, or in the mess hall, leaving only the platoon goldbrick, Private Mulvaney, who happened to be mowing dandelions when the attack took place.

But what have we now? Another passage backward through time, as at the Beacon Theatre? Well, yes and no. On the one hand, there appears to be a squad of soldiers marching—maybe ambling would be more accurate—around from behind one of the barracks. On the other hand, there is something not entirely convincing—in a military sense, that is—about the detachment. Furthermore, here, standing in the back of a slowly moving, vaguely Army-style truck, is none other than Buzz Sawyer, quite dashing with his blond hair blowing in the wind, and clearly pleased with himself, for he is smiling and pointing into the back of the truck, where four telephone booths are lying on their sides, like coffins.

"I got four booths!" he calls. "Where do you want them?"

"Stop right there," says Steve Horn. He turns to Ron Palazzo and says, "What am I supposed to do with four booths? I only need two."

"Hang on to them," says Palazzo. "You never know when they'll come in handy."

As the crew sets up in the middle of the deserted street outside one of the barracks, Palazzo busies himself with the task of keeping the talent in line and out of the way, the talent consisting of thirteen soldier types: one actor, who plays the recruit phoning his dad, the barber; and twelve extras, who play fellow-recruits. "O.K., guys," says Palazzo. "Go back in the barracks and get your gear looking right."

Vincent, who is taking light-level readings, and, naturally, is stripped to his undershirt, in keeping with the stiffness of the wind, pauses to remark: "Ron, you got some fine troops there."

Palazzo looks at Vincent and scowls briefly. He says, "I been in the Army. I know all about what crap it is."

"You were in the Army?" says Vincent. "In Nam?"

"Damn right I was in Nam," says Palazzo. "I was a captain."

"A captain?" says Vincent.

"Damn right," says Palazzo. "Only, I turned against the war. I marched against the war while I was in uniform. I was discharged as a private."

141

"The war was crap," says Vincent.

"Nobody knows that as well as me," says Palazzo. "That goddam Army. I enlisted. Nobody knows as well as me what crap that war was."

Inside the nearby barracks, a curious scene is in progress. Three members of the film crew are standing in front of one of the bare walls tossing coins at the baseboard—presumably enjoying a union-sponsored coin-tossing break. The twelve extras, each of them supposed to simulate a Marine recruit, right down to a nearly shaved head—although clearly they are *not* Marine recruits, for among other things, they seem to have a general delicacy of voice or manner—are standing about the empty room, or sitting on packing cases, discussing, for the most part, their agents.

"I mean to tell you, an agent is definitely important," says Paul, a youthful extra, almost completely shorn of hair, whose Marine jacket is in the process of being pinned up in back by Joanna Dendel. "But I think the *best* investment I ever made was going to school."

"Acting school?" says Joanna.

"Definitely acting school," says Paul. "But for commercials. Commercial school. It was a very important step for me. Very significant."

"What did they teach you?" says Joanna. "Turn around and stretch your arms."

Paul turns and stretches his arms. "Well, you know, it's not easy to put into words, but I would say the main thing they teach you is how to read copy," he says. "I mean, a lot of guys go into an audition and the casting guy hands them a sheet of copy and they don't know what to do with it. Sometimes they hold it too low and so they're looking down at it all the time. Or they look around for a table they can put it on and there's no table. Either way, they waste valuable time and they don't get themselves across. So—what commercial school teaches you, for one thing, is where to hold your copy. You hold it right up *here,* and *flat.* Flat is very important, because if you hold it right up here, you only have to move your eyes a very little bit, not even really dropping them, just moving them a very little bit—see how I do it?"

"That's very interesting," says Joanna. "You can turn back here now."

"The school really helped me a lot," says the extra. "I'd recommend it to anyone who was interested in getting into the business. Also, it taught me confidence. I wasn't nearly so confident before. I didn't really know how I looked to anyone else, because I'd never seen myself on camera."

Meanwhile, standing on the steps of the barracks, square-shouldered, also short of hair but with a well-fitted uniform and a generally all-American-boy appearance that make him seem a much more plausible Marine than his colleagues inside, is the principal talent, Eddie Dolphin by name, whose soldierly appearance is now somewhat fragmented by the arrival of Richard Hartenstein, with makeup kit, who begins dabbing at Dolphin's cheeks with a pad of rouge.

143

"I'm a guy who has a good time and don't let things bother him," says Eddie Dolphin. "Take these commercials. They're fun. I make some dough. I have a ball. I started doin' 'em after my dad was laid off and we were short of money. Two of my sisters did them, too. They're real cute. When you do commercials, you meet lots of interesting people and you go to lots of interesting places. I started really workin' more after my mom and dad were divorced and my mom didn't have too much money. I mean, you do what you can, right? But I'm lucky. I go to Fairleigh Dickinson University, in New Jersey, where I have a wrestling scholarship, and they don't hassle me about doin' these commercials. They're real nice to me there. And these commercial guys like Steve Horn are real nice to me, too. I'm a young guy, I'm having a ball. Last month, I shot a Coke ad with Steve. I'm the guy with the long hair flying who wipes out on the motorcycle. I really have a good time in life. I never get too intense, if you know what I mean. I go to a lot of different places, like Florida. I make good money. I'm my family's sole support right now, but don't think I don't enjoy life, don't think I don't go partyin'. I'd say there ain't a week I don't go partyin', havin' myself a ball. But imagine me partyin' with my hair this short!"

Now Palazzo appears, striding up the steps, nodding to Eddie Dolphin, entering the barracks, clipboard in hand, and wearing, as it happens, an old Army jacket. "O.K., guys," he says, with a not too subtle hint of distaste in his voice. "Let's shape up this squad!"

The extras look around them in disbelief and confusion. "What do you want us to do?" says one of them.

"I want you to stand tall," says Palazzo.

The extras shuffle into a vague approximation of military line.

"Jesus, you men gotta maintain the gig line," says Palazzo, walking down in front of them. "Come on, belts and buttons lined up."

"*Lined up?*" says one of the extras.

"You heard me, guy," says Palazzo. "Belts and buttons lined up. You got to look like soldiers, don't you? Some of these boots need shining. You, over there! That brass looks pretty bad."

"You a technical adviser?" says one of the extras.

"Damn right I'm a technical adviser," says Palazzo. He turns to Gaston, who has just arrived and is studying the unusual military group with the wary eye of a former French Army conscript. "Look, the Army isn't worth a goddam," Palazzo says, "but I can't let these guys go out looking like this, can I?"

"I think they're ready out front," says Gaston. "Do we need guns?"

"Rifles—never guns," says Palazzo. "Not for recruits."

"I always thought guns," says Gaston. "Guns and butter."

Outside on the street, Steve Horn and company have the lights in place and the camera in place and the phone booths in place. Steve Horn says to Jerry Pfiffner: "I'm trying to decide which look we want—a marching look or a kind of hanging-around-the-phone-booth look."

"Marching might be more Marine," says Pfiffner, "but it may not read."

Now there is the sound of cadence-calling—"Hup, two, three, four"—and the squad of extras appears around the corner of the barracks, with Palazzo on the flank. Palazzo brings them along past the phone booths and stops them just in front of Steve and his camera. "O.K. Stop!" says Palazzo, in a newfound, or rediscovered, parade-ground voice. "Men, 'tenshun! Hands and arms at your sides." One of the extras slips a hand into his pocket. "Guys, I said hands and arms at your sides. That's right, arms straight, fists lightly clenched. This isn't the goddam British Army." He turns to Steve. "Steve, here's your squad," he says.

"That's very nice, Palazzo," says Steve. "Did I hear you say 'Stop'?"

"Jesus!" says Palazzo. "Did I say 'Stop'?"

"I was a 4-F—only I know you don't say 'Stop' in the Army. You say—"

"O.K., guys," says Palazzo. "I should have said 'Halt.' From now on, when I say 'Halt' you stop."

Two and a half hours later, when the shooting is over, and Steve has filmed both the marching look and the hanging-around-the-phone-booth look and a couple of looks in between, he takes Linda and Gaston and Jerry on a bumpy, bizarrely pastoral drive in the station wagon, past the dune grasses, along a little coastal dirt road toward the concrete outcroppings in the distance, which turn out to be the remains of Second World War gun emplacements. At a seemingly randomly selected spot along the windblown coast, everyone gets out and has a look around.

"Imagine all this being out here!" says Steve, gazing up at a large concrete pillbox, almost overgrown with sea grasses. "Imagine them trying to defend New York Harbor."

"This is just what the Germans had in Normandy," says Gaston.

"But imagine these guns being right *here,* guarding New York from attack," says Steve. "It gives you goose bumps."

"Come on, guys," says Linda. "The sand is blowing everywhere. Have you had your fun?"

Back in the car, Jerry says: "Steve, I guess you just like to drive around."

"I guess I do, all right," says Steve, turning the station wagon in the sandy road. "You know, driving always has a nice feel for me, even in traffic. One of the things I remember from long ago—it must have been right after the war: my dad would take us all out driving on the Belt Parkway every Sunday. Every Sunday afternoon, we'd all get in the car, and he'd drive us up and down and around the goddam Belt Parkway. I guess it was his idea of a family thing to do. I guess he also really loved that road."

Trouble in the Dailies

JERRY SPOTS THE TROUBLE FIRST, WHILE GASTON IS off in a corner making a phone call to tell his wife that he will be late for dinner, and while Steve is out of the room attending to some office business. It is early evening, and the three men (for Linda is dealing with bills in the front area, and Elliott has taken the train back to Long Island) have gathered in Steve's conference room to view the "dailies" on a little movie screen—the dailies being the takes from previous days' shooting which have been sent to be developed and have recently been returned.

What Jerry has spotted is what seems to be a flaw, an error, a problem, something not quite right, in the scene of the black girl doing a yoga headstand.

"She's down too far," he says as Gaston comes back from the phone.

They run the film back. "I don't see it," Gaston says.

"Her head," says Jerry. "She's not resting on her head, she's on her forehead."

"You can't see the top of her face," says Gaston.

"The phone doesn't look right," says Jerry.

Gaston goes to find Steve, who is conferring with Joanna about the hockey-shirt emblem. "Lightning is good," Steve says. On a piece of scratch paper, he draws a zigzag line representing a bolt of lightning.

"A small bolt?" says Joanna.

"Not too small," says Steve. "We want it to show, right? Look here, Gaston, we got our team—the Lightnings."

"I like it," says Gaston. "I think we have a problem with the black yoga."

Steve goes back to the conference room, and they replay the black yoga takes.

"She's rolling over on her face," says Steve.

"You see too much chin," says Jerry.

"Is it that way in all the takes?" says Steve.

"Just about," says Jerry. "It spoils the look."

"I knew we were going to have problems with that girl," says Steve. "Don't ask me why. A hunch. I should have seen the head rolling forward."

"It's very subtle," says Jerry. "It's subtle, but it's wrong."

"It magnifies," says Gaston.

"I should have seen it," says Steve.

"Nobody saw it," says Jerry. "Besides, we were all worrying about the cat."

"O.K.," says Steve. "We have no choice. We reshoot."

"We reshoot," says Jerry.

"The schedule's awful tight," says Gaston.

"Don't worry—I'll fit it in after the rodeo," says Steve. "But without the cat."

Bring On the Bulls

THE DAY AFTER FORT TILDEN, STEVE HORN AND HIS troops drive south along the rain-soaked New Jersey Turnpike, at first through fumes of chemicals and then past the barren environs of Fort Dix and later, with the rain beginning to lift and with fields of damp, dark green showing on either side, into soft, dull farmland, which stretches down across the nearby Delaware border, and which contains, as surely one of South Jersey's most improbable points of interest, the grounds of Cowtown Rodeo. On this particular morning, with the crew already in somewhat low spirits because of the rain and several missed turnoffs as a result of malfunctioning walkie-talkie equipment, the rodeo grounds seem to have been already taken over by the forces of Winston cigarettes, if not in person, at least in sign and spirit, for as the cars and vans and trucks circle the rather dilapidated rodeo arena, what is most in evidence, aside from evil-looking mud and yellow puddles, is a succession of bright-red Winston-cigarette posters, placards, banners, and so forth, which appear to be hanging from every available corral pole and bleacher seat.

"Those cigarette people are everywhere," says Gaston Braun, his aesthetic distaste clearly at war with sound mercantile admiration.

"So this is Winston Country," says Elliott Manketo. "I knew it was somewhere."

Steve Horn is slogging about in the muddy stockade area with Vincent, Loet Farkas, and Ron Palazzo, looking for a place to set up. "This is a gutsy little place," he says. "I can do things here. Thank God for the new lights, though—the H.M.I.s. A few years ago, you couldn't work on this kind of day at all; you'd have to stay home when it rained, or shoot inside. But outside on a rainy day now, with the H.M.I.s, it's almost better, in a way, because you have less contrast—the scene is softer, more beautiful."

At this moment, as if playing the part of homesteaders walking out to offer a wary welcome to the newly arrived cavalry, three men come forward across the arena, each one with an unmistakably Western or cowboy look to him, traceable to the broad-brimmed cowboy hats, the jeans, and the boots—but whose effect is somewhat offset, on closer inspection, by three shiny red windbreakers advertising Winston cigarettes. The youngest of the three men is the present owner of Cowtown, Grant Harris: an easygoing, friendly fellow in his twenties, born and raised, as it turns out, in New

Jersey, though he now possesses a fine Rocky Mountain accent.

"It's a terrific spread," says Steve Horn.

The three men look at him with the dour innocence, doubtless, of men who do not know they are wearing windbreakers advertising Winston cigarettes.

"If you say so," says Grant.

"I do," says Steve. "I think the light is going to be very good, very soft. But I don't see any bulls."

One of the two older men in windbreakers says: "Nobody said anything about bulls."

Steve turns to Vincent. "Didn't we say bulls?"

"Don't ask me," says Vincent.

Grant says: "How many bulls do you need?"

"Jesus, I don't want a lot of them," says Steve. "I mean, I want to put this cowboy over there, and then I want to see some bulls behind him."

"Doin' *what?*" says the other older man.

"I don't know," says Steve. "Whatever bulls do."

"O.K., I'll get you some bulls," says Grant.

"The kind with horns," says Steve as Grant starts to leave. "I need to see horns."

"Horns is what you'll git," says Grant, with a twang.

The bulls, however, don't seem instantly accessible, for Grant is observed riding sedately off across a series of low, tree-studded hills on the far side of the rodeo arena. Also, the rain has started to come down again in earnest, so Steve and the group repair to the nearby Cowtown Restaurant, whose interior contains a drab coffee-shop counter—behind which hangs a large notice

announcing last summer's South Jersey Tractor Pull—
and has a small room to the side, decorated with animal horns and rodeo posters, where most of the extras
are sitting, having coffee, eating pastry, and talking, as
usual, about their agents. Behind this is a smaller
room, littered with what seem to be discarded auto
parts (perhaps the wreckage from the South Jersey
Tractor Pull) , where Steve's cowboy is being costumed
and some of the extras are exchanging Western belts
and neckerchiefs and hats among themselves in order
to achieve the most satisfactory fit. Today, there are
also some female extras: three girls, quite cute and
pretty, though too soft of face and fluffy of eye to be
easily mistaken for genuine cowgirls. The cowboy extras also seem somewhat delicate for their roles; with
them, however, it is less a matter of too much softness,
let us say, as of an almost palpable absence of Western
simplicity or "weight." Still, there is no denying that
with the addition of Western gear—especially the hats
—they have achieved the *look*.

Three of the cowboy extras, newly costumed, are
seated at a table with one of the cowgirls.

"June, you should *not* wear that scarf," says one of
the cowboys. "Not with the pink plaid."

"It's the only one they had left," says the cowgirl.

"Better no scarf than *that* scarf," says the cowboy.

Seated at the counter in the main part of the restaurant, Steve Horn, who, despite his Brooklyn origins,
is clearly the only genuine Westerner in Cowtown that
morning, drinks coffee with Linda, Gaston, and Jerry

—who is writing and crossing out "Reach Out" lyrics in a little notebook.

A large woman frying eggs behind the counter says: "You people with the television?"

Steve looks up but is silent.

Linda says: "We make television commercials."

"Is that easy work?" the woman says. "I could use some easy work."

Steve looks up again. "It's all in the lighting," he says. "It's one hundred per cent in the lighting."

"That's all it is—lighting?" says the woman.

Steve gets to his feet and walks toward the door. "I think I hear the bulls," he says.

Linda pays for the coffee as Gaston follows Steve outside, and Jerry stays behind, like a kid with his homework not yet finished. In the distance, several hundred yards away, trotting down out of the trees on the hillside, with many a whoop and a holler, rides Grant, driving a half-dozen bulls ahead of him.

Soon the setting-up work resumes, with the downpour fading again to drizzle, with many umbrellas mushrooming over the lights, with much mud underfoot, and with a stirring display of carpentry by Tommy Drohan, who fashions a simulated shack or hut out of one of the bucking chutes, in which he then hangs a black wall phone on a nail. Now the cowboy, an actor named Preston Brown, assumes his place in the little shack and practices his telephone technique. Now three of the six bulls appear, formidably shuffling down one of the sorting pens; also, in a smaller corral to one side, a dozen or so horses are driven in by the two older men in windbreakers.

"That's beautiful," Steve says, glancing up from his camera. "That's really great." He turns to Gaston. "You know, you could never do this in California. Can you imagine asking for six bulls in California?"

While Gaston is considering an appropriate reply, Linda appears from yet another direction, leading the cowboys and cowgirls—ten of them. "Where do you want them?" she calls.

"Arrange them along the fence," Steve says.

Gaston says: "Where are the numbers?"

Steve says: "Linda, do we have the numbers? People in rodeos have numbers on their backs."

Joanna steps forward with an armful of white cloth squares that have numbers on them, and these are distributed to the extras.

"Are those regulation numbers?" says Steve.

"Actually, they're Olympic track numbers," says Linda. "We used them in the Coke ad. Remember, we tried to get real rodeo numbers from the City Center —you know, they do that ballet *Rodeo*—but it didn't work out."

"They're terrific," says Steve. "Except maybe we should dirty them up a bit."

Preston Brown, the cowboy, is talking to a member of the crew. "Man, this is a big break for me, working in this job," he says. "I came from San Francisco two years ago, I had this one job for Pabst, but then I had a real personal disaster. I mean, it really brought me down, man. I was doing this job for Pan Am—I mean, I was in it, they filmed it—and then there was the Screen Actors Guild strike and they scrapped the commercial. It was just a goddam personal disaster."

"Cowboy, are you ready now?" says Steve.

"Sure am," says Preston Brown, fluffing out his hair a little below his hat. "A guy's gotta get back on his horse. Right?"

"Grant, you ready with those bulls?" says Steve.

Grant waves a hand and calls: "You better get those guys up on top of that fence when the bulls go by."

"O.K., cowboys and cowgirls, move up to the top of that fence," says Steve.

There is a moment of silence.

"Say when you're ready," says Grant. "I can't keep these bulls back forever."

One of the extras calls in a loud voice to another: "Tony, are you going to Fire Island next weekend?"

Steve says: "O.K., everyone up on the fence! And remember, remember, everyone, we want *rodeo*, not *farm*. Camera! Action! Bring on the bulls!"

A couple of hours later, when the vignette is finished (it did not go badly, except that Preston Brown had a tendency to wince every time one of the bulls passed near him, and except that for the first hour most of the extras were seated facing the wrong direction), Steve and the group stop along the road for ice cream before getting back on the turnpike for the return trip to the city. Everyone is fairly subdued—or, at least, quiet—except for Gaston, who is trying, without any luck, to obtain a beer from the waitress.

"Is this a dry state?" he asks the girl, who is about sixteen and is dressed in a sort of Dutch-girl ensemble.

"Do you mean does it *rain*, or what?" says the girl.

"Gaston, nobody has beer with ice cream," says Jerry Pfiffner.

Steve says: "You know, I said it was one hundred per cent in the lighting, but that doesn't account for personal style. I mean, to be a top guy in the business you have to have a personal style—not so it actually sticks out at you and says 'style,' but so it's there, it's *you*. I figure my style is the telephoto lens. You know, years ago I used wide-angle all the time, like with those soap ads when you have a couple of women, up close, looking right at the camera, and a box of soap drops over their shoulders and that's all you see. But I got tired of that. It's limited, isn't it? All those big boxes. So I use telephoto. I think it gives you an effect that's less commercial and more real. Not *really* real, but more real than commercial. I think you could say telephoto is my style."

All Vignetted Out

And now the final day of shooting on "Tap Dancing": a three-vignette day—or, at any rate, a two-and-a-half, the two vignettes consisting of the girl jockey and the toothless hockey player, and the half being a reshoot of the black-girl yoga. The morning is hot and humid, even at dawn, when the working day begins. First come the usual milling around and loading, and then a trip into the exurbs of Westchester, where some private horse-show grounds have been reserved for filming the girl-jockey vignette—though, as an accommodation to the new location, which is certainly greener and prettier than most race tracks, the part has been changed to an equestrienne. The girl chosen for the role, clearly more model than actress, is stunningly pretty and also friendly and businesslike; and, with the ambience of contrived elegance around the horse-show ring, with a handful of huge, temporarily docile hunters discreetly paraded in the background, and with a batch of new extras—different extras, male and female; older, perhaps, and wiser—togged out in queen's-garden-party finery, the shooting goes surprisingly well and fast, and there is a feeling of casual high spirits among the members of the crew, many of whom have, predictably, stripped to the waist to take advantage of the Westchester sunshine.

Steve Horn seems to be unusually relaxed himself, as if he had imbibed some of the garden-party atmosphere from his set, though he is definitely not stripped to the waist; on the contrary, he is wearing a loose and lineny outfit of beige shirt and beige slacks, very cool and flowing and somewhat pukka-sahib, though whether in private deference to Westchester horse country or out of a desire to put Cowtown behind him it is hard to tell.

Jerry, who is wearing his standard costume of sports shirt and Levi's—always real, no-nonsense Levi's, worn in what is perhaps some noble Iowa manner: unfaded, unsoftened, and unbelled at the bottoms—remarks admiringly on Steve's change of appearance.

"You know, three years ago everything I had was dungarees," says Steve. "But then I threw them all out. I lost interest in dungarees. But I tell you it's not so easy to find a substitute. This morning, I guess you might say I'm very Calvin Klein."

There is a slight delay while one of the big hunters, doubtless having grown restive at the constant parading back and forth to no obvious gain of his own, is calmed down by a tiny groom. Tricia, the pretty girl, in tan breeches, green jacket, and velvet equestrienne hat, is having her few exquisite beads of sweat removed by Richard Hartenstein.

"I'd say that's definitely a California look," says Linda.

Steve says: "I think it's more universal than California. Like Cheryl Tiegs. Cheryl started as a California look, but she became more universal."

Linda says to Jerry: "We used Cheryl long ago. I mean, before she was Cheryl Tiegs. Also Travolta. We used Travolta very early, when he was just a kid with a few moves."

Jerry says: "I guess California has an awful lot of talent, though I'm not sure it has most of the acting."

Steve says: "Well, New York is the only place if you want the New York look. A couple of months ago, this ad-agency guy called me up—we were casting some country barbecue scene—and he says, 'Let's not have the New York look.' I said, 'You mean you don't want anybody Jewish or Italian?' He said, 'I guess that's what I mean.' "

Linda says: "I'm Irish, and people say I have a New York look."

"*Irish* isn't the New York look," says Steve.

In about two hours, the equestrienne vignette is completed, and then the entire crew, except for the pretty girl with the universal look and the extras with the garden-party look, drives over to Greenwich, Connecticut, where a house has been found in which to re-shoot the black yoga scene. There is a new black yoga girl, smaller and somewhat quieter of manner than the first one; also yellow running shorts; also no cat lady and no cat.

"I miss the cat," says Gaston. "It was a touch."

"It was a touch," says Jerry, "but it never really worked."

"The baby worked," says Gaston.

"We can't stick a baby in every vignette," says Jerry.

Gaston says: "No, I mean, it's a funny thing the baby worked and the cat didn't."

The black yoga shooting also seems to be proceeding with relative smoothness, though a problem has appeared on the horizon, in the person of Bryan Trottier, the star center of the New York Islanders hockey team, who had apparently agreed to play the toothless hockey player in the afternoon's vignette but whose "business representative" has now phoned to say that Bryan is scheduled to make a public appearance at a Long Island shopping center and so may be delayed awhile.

"What's 'delayed awhile'?" says Steve.

"That's what the business representative said," says Alayne.

"Look, it's Bryan's first commercial, isn't it?" says Steve. "He wanted it. He wanted to do his first commercial for us. And now this guy calls and says he'll be 'delayed awhile.' Doesn't he know we booked Shea Stadium?"

"I'll try to reach him," says Alayne.

"You can't phone a person at a shopping center," says Steve.

What is a bit odd about the yoga-headstand scene (all the yoga-headstand scenes), though it is perhaps not worth mentioning, perhaps rather too indelicate or somehow difficult to mention, is that the essential subject of the scene—and not merely the scene on film but the scene as it is being shot on location—is a young woman wearing only a brief, skintight equivalent of a body stocking and positioned upside down in a very definite manner, with her legs bent outward from what might be called the groin, forming a V or triangle. It is, of course, a classic gymnastic posture; indeed, a classic yoga posture. It is, however—perhaps to take too dim a view of human nature—a scene that might cause surreptitious giggles among schoolboys (doubtless schoolgirls as well) and evil leers among disgusting old gentlemen; it is a scene with a certain odd, though undeniable, focus to it. But the fact is that throughout today's shooting, as in the earlier yoga scenes, at the Zacharia house, there is scarcely any indication from any source—not even from the youthful and laid-back crew—that there is anything unusual or arresting in the young woman's posture, or, more to the point, that there is anything intended or suggested by such a pose. The only hint, as it happens, that prurient possibilities might conceivably be lurking in the basic design comes from a young gaffer, who observes, within Elliott's earshot, that the girl (and maybe certain aspects of her pose) might be worthy of *Playboy*.

"That's ridiculous," says Elliott.

"She sure looks good upside down," says the gaffer.

"Jesus, it's yoga!" says Elliott. "Housewives are doing this stuff all over the country."

"No *kidding,*" says the gaffer.

Around one-thirty, after the usual catered repast of salad, cold cuts, the obligatory hot dish of beef Stroganoff (some days disguised as spaghetti Stroganoff, some days as shrimp Stroganoff), and, today, a huge and peculiar bright-yellow gelatine dessert, the gang packs up, leaves Greenwich, and heads toward the city, veering left over the Triborough Bridge toward La-Guardia Airport and then Shea Stadium. The parking lot at Shea is empty but is seemingly impenetrable. Steve, in the station wagon, followed by the vans and then the trucks, drives several times around the encircling wire fence, the walkie-talkies sputtering with static and well-meant inaccurate advice. Steve himself attempts to maintain a dignified leadership demeanor, though he is in the position of a general who has arrived to take over the palace in a coup, only to find that the caretaker has locked the gates and left for the day. Finally, however, an entrance is found, the vehicles are parked, and the crew begins hauling gear into the catacomblike recesses of the large, ugly stadium.

The place chosen for the hockey-vignette filming is the visiting players' changing room: a square, low-ceilinged chamber of ample size, neither attractive nor unattractive, neither notably locker-roomish nor especially chic. In fact, in keeping with the progressive nature of modern sports, the four walls are lined not with lockers but with stalls, each containing a bench, some hooks, and an overhead shelf. A dull-green heavy-duty carpet covers the floor; there are some tables, chairs, a laundry hamper; and now the lights and camera gear; and now the extras, several of whom are clearly veterans of the rodeo vignette in Cowtown. As the extras arrive, they are given contracts to sign by Ron Palazzo, and hockey gear and uniforms by Joanna, who has miraculously contrived to produce a dozen or so complete hockey outfits—shoulder pads, elbow pads, shin guards, appropriately cut-off long underwear, skates, sticks, headgear, black nylon shorts, and splendid red shirts with an emblem, sewn on each, of a bolt of lightning.

One of the new extras, a beefy fellow of soft, ample girth, starts putting on his gear with the assurance of a pro.

"I think those elbow pads go on the other way," says Ron Palazzo.

"They cut off the circulation like that," says the extra.

"Let's do it by the book," says Palazzo.

The extra shrugs and readjusts the elbow pads, observing to a nearby colleague, who is studying his contract, "I been living in sports equipment all week. We was up in Mount Vernon doing a football commercial for Coke. You ever see this guy Mean Joe Greene, from Pittsburgh or somewhere? A big guy, very big. I had to stand around for two days, you know, *huddling*, with this damn helmet on my head, and then when the ball was snapped I'd hand Mean Joe Greene a Coke."

"You get any calls for 7Up?" says the other extra, who is tall and skinny, and who arrived wearing a skintight work shirt and a Levi jacket. "I hear they're using athlete types."

"I don't mind the *huddling*," says the beefy extra, "but I hate those helmets. You don't suppose we have helmets today?"

Steve has been pacing back and forth, with Jerry, and then with Gaston, and then with Linda, waiting for the arrival of the one genuine athlete in the assembly, Bryan Trottier, when the door of the changing room opens and in walk, first, a large, florid, middle-aged man, wearing checked trousers and a brown jacket; and, next, a somewhat shorter, younger man, wearing a dark pin-striped suit, a striped tie with tiepin, and black Gucci loafers, and carrying a briefcase; and, finally, a young man of more or less medium size, with a round and almost soft pale face, wearing a light-blue leisure suit and carrying a hockey stick. Steve walks over to greet Bryan Trottier, the soft-faced young man with the hockey stick, kidding him genially about the Islanders' unlucky venture in the recent semifinals. Trottier responds in a voice as soft as his features, trying to be friendly but clearly a young man of few words. Not so his colleagues—the man in the checked trousers and the man in the Gucci loafers, who are, respectively, Bryan Trottier's agent and his business manager.

When Palazzo comes over to hand Trottier the standard contract, the agent quickly takes it, then hands Palazzo a sheaf of papers. "Here's *your* contract," he says.

Palazzo glances at the papers and stuffs them in his back pocket. "This is quite an honor," he says dourly, "having you guys come out here."

"I come to the big ones," says the agent. "Let me tell you, most of the agents in New York are a bunch of bums. Did you hear that? *Bums.* They never leave their offices, and so they die early."

The business manager is talking with Jerry Pfiffner. "This is a big day for Bryan," he says. "It's his first commercial. Don't get me wrong, I don't mean it's a big day like winning the playoffs, but it's a big day in terms of the over-all career. We think Bryan has very big potential in sales and image—in credibility. Of course, the competition is fierce. There's no denying that. Bryan is very realistic about the competition. He realizes that although he's definitely a superstar, he's not the *only* superstar."

"Well, he's still pretty young," says Jerry.

"Very young," says the business manager, "but young with credibility."

Trottier himself is seated in front of one of the stalls donning the hockey gear. He is surrounded by his new teammates, who, bizarrely, with their spiffy red sweaters and pads, manage somehow to look more *athletic* than the Islanders center. When he is fully dressed, he carefully removes his two front teeth and puts them away in a little box.

"I bet that hurt when it happened," Linda says.

Trottier looks embarrassed but smiles shyly. "Actually, it didn't hurt at all," he says. Then: "I was playing junior hockey in Canada and got hit by a stick. I didn't really feel a thing." Then a real torrent of words: "I didn't have them fixed for a long time, but I got them fixed now, so I can take them out, because a lot of guys have them fixed so you can't take them out, they stay in place, which is good in a lot of ways—you know, more convenient—but it's not so good, of course, if you get hit in the teeth again." Then silence.

"I see," says Linda.

When the members of the team are all suited up, or, rather, suited down—for, since the scene is to be a post-game celebration, the extras have to be in various stages of modest undress—Steve rehearses them in the action of the vignette. The rehearsing is part crowd control and part ballet: two players move here; another player moves there and waves; two players go back and forth here; Bryan, the key player, comes from here, goes to the phone; another player passes him and douses him with champagne; another player douses the first douser; and so forth.

"O.K., guys," says Steve. "First, you gotta get wet, you gotta get into the showers and get wet. I need to see sweat. You've been playing a championship game and I need to see sweat."

As the extras follow Trottier into the showers, where Richard Hartenstein supervises the wetting, the beefy extra remarks, "I'm telling you, they didn't use showers on the Coke job, they gave us little spray things—very first-class."

Meanwhile, Mac McDaniel has arrived—an emissary from A.T.&T. Long Lines. He and Gaston and Jerry confer. Gaston then goes over to Steve. "Remember, we have to watch the drinking," he says.

"Jesus, you're absolutely right," Steve says. "O.K., team," he says. "Remember, we have no drinking the booze, absolutely no drinking from the cups, the glasses, no drinking if the stuff runs down your face, no drinking on camera, right? We all know the rules, right?"

With Steve operating the camera, and with Jerry, Gaston, and Elliott scanning the action on the video-tape screen, Trottier and his teammates on the victorious Lightnings go through their ballet of celebration, yelling, pushing, fizzing real bottles of New York State champagne, squirting champagne everywhere, while Trottier stands in the foreground, telephone to his ear, communicating with his toothless son, finishing with a big smile, a big wave of the fist, and a flash of teeth around the center gap. Again and again they go through it. Sometimes an extra falls down; sometimes one goes in the wrong direction; sometimes Trottier doesn't quite achieve the right smile.

Steve says: "Bryan, try to keep your mouth open."

Jerry says: "He's got to *extend* the laugh there."

Steve says: "Bryan, you got to hold the laugh and show me teeth."

They have done twenty-three takes, and the two cases of New York State champagne have run out and have been replaced by ginger ale poured into the champagne bottles and then, when the ginger ale has run out, by water.

Steve says: "Bryan, it's nice, it's beautiful, but I'd really like to see more teeth."

They get set for one more time, with Linda and Joanna refilling the champagne bottles.

"I love this feature stuff," says one of the extras. "What I hate is that product stuff—hanging around all day to make love to a box of Wheaties. But this feature stuff is like being in the movies."

Steve says: "Camera! Action! Let's make it beautiful!"

Once again, the Lightnings begin their carousing through the locker room while Trottier brandishes the phone, gets doused with water, beams, shows the gap in his teeth.

Steve says: "Bryan, extend the smile, *extend*." And: "Big grin." And: "Open wide." And: "Yes, yes, yes." And: "Guys, we got it."

Afterward, as the changing room empties out—with the extras leaving first, and then the parade of camera gear, and then Mac McDaniel walking out with Elliott, and Gaston with Jerry—Bryan Trottier, back in his leisure suit, stands silently behind his business manager, who is engaged in earnest monologue with Steve. "I represent the financial-management side," the man says. "Not just athletes. We got entertainers.

We got Mike Douglas. We got Stanley Siegel. We also got eight jockeys. We offer complete estate-planning services. We pay bills. We offer a complete financial line."

Trottier steps forward, almost like a young boy, and hands Steve a hockey stick, which he has apparently autographed to Steve. "In case you don't have one of mine," says Trottier.

"Bryan, that's really nice," says Steve. "That's really nice."

On his way across the parking lot with Linda, Jerry, and Gaston, Steve waves the autographed hockey stick at members of the crew, who are still loading up the trucks.

"He thinks he won the game," says Jerry.

Steve walks over to speak a few words to Vincent, whose walkie-talkie is beginning to crackle once again.

"You know, he's at the top right now," says Linda. "Steve, Levine, and Giraldi. He's at the peak. But in two years, or in a year, he could be way down. If something doesn't work out, it doesn't matter whose fault it really is, it's *your* fault. It's terrible, isn't it, to be so good at what you do, to be an artist in a business, when you're only as good as your last commercial."

Jerry says: "I don't think Steve has to worry."

Linda says: "I hope not. I hope he gets to enjoy the top for a while."

Steve returns to the station wagon, makes a few trial passes at Gaston with the hockey stick, then shoves it in the back of the car and climbs into the driver's seat. For a few seconds, he sits behind the steering wheel rubbing his eyes. "I guess I'm all vignetted out," he says. Then he smiles, pats Linda on the knee, starts up the car, and roars off to find the exit to the city.

Crisp and Tight

WITH THE SHOOTING ON THE VIGNETTES COM-pleted, Steve Horn's active involvement with the project has in fact come to an end, although work on the commercial is still far from over. No formal cere-mony of leave-taking occurs—no farewell leis are ex-changed by members of the Horn organization and the union hands, or even by Steve and Linda Horn and the Ayer people—which is strange in a way, since the various parties have been journeying, as it were, at close quarters for many days, but is probably not so remarkable in that the piecework, communal nature of the business makes it likely that sooner or later many of the individuals will be working with one an-other once again. Even so, among the survivors there is a subtle air, not of anything so extreme as abandon-ment, but perhaps of temporarily diminished vigor. For while Steve Horn and his merry men have van-ished into the night, so to speak, taking with them their trucks, vans, lights, cables, bagels, and little canapés of ham and pineapple, "Tap Dancing" remains: twenty metal cans containing roughly ten thousand feet of processed film from which forty-five feet must be extracted for the final commercial.

"I wonder where Steve is today," says Gaston.

"On Long Island, I think," says Jerry. "He's shooting Burger King."

"I thought he didn't like products," says Elliott.

"Burger King isn't exactly a *product*," says Jerry.

The three Ayer men are waiting in one of the editing rooms in Take 5 Productions, on East Fifty-fifth Street, for Howie Lazarus, the film editor, to begin work on the uncut footage. Take 5 is a busy and typically unprepossessing establishment: an office of a half-dozen rooms mainly occupied by machinery, though not the big, brutish machinery of the bygone industrial era but, rather, the lighter, sense-oriented machinery of the new communications age. Everywhere, there are screens for viewing: small screens, medium screens, large screens. In each room, strips of film hang from baskets, with an air of carefree abundance, as in a market. In each room, too, there is at least one Moviola machine, and sometimes two: gray-green contraptions with outstretched spindly metal arms, not unlike those of a dentist's drill. Also film-splicing machines, somewhat larger than those they sell for home movies but still relatively modest and unelaborate—insufficient, it might seem, for serious work. There are no chairs in evidence; no real chairs,

174

that is—only a couple of metal stools. In short, little
deference to general comfort, or even to client comfort. There are some shelves against the wall, but no
books—only metal cans of film with labels such as
"Liberty Mutual," "Wells Rich Greene," "Bob and
Ray," "Corning Glass," and "Sperry Rand," and a
great many reading "A.T.&T."

Howie Lazarus now begins playing through the first
takes on his Moviola. A reel of film spins on the machine—which actually sounds rather like an old-fashioned dentist's drill—and a small, bright-colored
picture shows up on a viewing screen to the side.

At first, the moment seems magical. A lesson in the
wonders of photography—those pictures of the bear
in Yellowstone that actually came out! Here, now, in
the middle of the Moviola screen, is the little girl in
the red-white-and-blue costume (what was her name?
Tiffany Blake) dancing her heart out while her stage
mommy, a vague presence, beams in the background,
and her stage daddy, also peripheral, sits on the floor
holding the telephone.

"That has a nice quality," says Gaston. "Crisp."

"I think we can get crisper," says Jerry.

The take is over in a matter of seconds. Then there
is another one, just like it—or *is* it just like it?

"This is crisp," says Gaston.

"It's tight," says Jerry.

"More back light," says Howie. "I'd rather drift in
on the other one."

As the numerous takes parade through the Moviola, Howie periodically stops the machine, reels the film back manually, and makes a crayon mark—a big squiggle—on one of the frames. In fact, film editing, in Howie's hands, seems to be a process that is self-assured to the point of being strangely casual. For instance, as he spins the reel on the Moviola forward and backward, ribbons of film begin to unwind onto the floor, which he shoves out of the way with his shoe, or picks up and dumps unceremoniously onto a nearby table, the film seemingly all in a tangle, looping and crisscrossing this way and that way, until he grabs what might or might not be one of the ends and yanks it back into some kind of order. Howie deals with film, one imagines, in somewhat the fashion of a Navajo mother dealing with her children—cuffing them, or dropping them, or forgetting them, so that an outsider begins to worry: how will they ever survive this treatment? But actually the offhandedness of the process is deceptive—based on a careful accommodation to fairly precise tolerances—and survival is rarely at issue, or so one hopes.

Now Howie and his three companions are looking at the takes from the recently reshot black yoga: a black girl upside down—her legs triangled in midscreen—with a telephone next to her face.

Elliott says: "This is tight."

Jerry says: "I'd say we need it tighter."

Howie says: "Tighter is no problem, but the telephone doesn't read."

Another take is run through.

Gaston says: "I'm not sure about the feet."

Jerry says: "You can't see the feet."

Gaston says: "That's what I mean. They should be crossed."

Elliott says: "Crossed isn't standard."

Another take.

Jerry says: "You can see the feet, but it isn't tight."

Gaston says: "I don't mean tightly crossed. A little crossed."

Elliott says: "Crossed is gymnastics."

Gaston says: "Not a *little* crossed."

As if he had just spotted or remembered something, Howie suddenly reels back the spool of film, then reels it forward again, then kicks an unwanted loop out of his way, then leans over the machine and makes another crayon squiggle on a frame. "That one reads telephone," he says.

Shooting into the Sun and

Other Techniques

I<small>N THE COURSE OF THE NEXT WEEK</small>, H<small>OWIE</small> L<small>AZARUS</small> becomes the new source of energy for the commercial. He is not such a commanding figure as Steve Horn, or, at least, not so physically imposing; he is an amiable, somewhat rumpled man of forty-five, of middle height, with tousled, sandy hair and a matter-of-fact, even offhand manner. But the hours he works seem just as long, and if the type of energy he provides is less dramatic—has fewer flourishes—it appears to be fully as necessary to the completion of the project. In this sense, the word "editing" in the phrase "film editing" is probably something of a misnomer, for to the layman it implies the sort of modest rearranging or simple excision that for generations has obtained in the world of writing and print. But the fact is—and this is perhaps where the various *auteur* claims of screen directors, screenwriters, and so on inevitably founder— that Howie's work on "Tap Dancing," while no *more* authorial than Steve Horn's or Jerry Pfiffner's, is in certain ways no *less* authorial. The material that Howie has to work with is still close to the "raw" stage: those thousands of feet of film, whose tens of thousands of frames contain expressions, gestures, shades of light, tones of color—all of them a duplication that is not quite a duplication—and which are still, as it were, malleable. Over the past two days, Howie has virtually completed the rough cut, whereby the five vignettes have been reduced from an average of twenty-five takes each to four or five takes. Now he is working on the final cut: winding, unwinding, marking, splicing, sometimes resplicing, continually kicking aside loops of the sinuous, glistening, for the most part obedient film.

"I can't say I really aimed at being a film editor," says Howie. "I was a young guy studying to be an accountant. It seemed to make sense then to want to be an accountant—you know, steady work, good money, a solid place in the community. But I never quite made it into the profession, I guess mostly because I started doing part-time work for one of the big commercial-production companies, called Transfilm, and I just sort of stayed in the business. This was twenty-seven years ago, and let me say that the whole business of filming commercials has changed radically since then. In those days, the big shops did everything: they did the directing, the editing, the animation, the optical stuff. I guess they were like the big studios in the heyday of Hollywood. There were big people in those days, with big visions. They were going to do it all. But then some of the guys just started to splinter off. There was definitely a splintering process. The directors started to splinter off. The editors started to splinter off. I guess it was like what happened with the movie studios. One day, there was size and scale—everything under one roof. The next day, there were a lot of different shops. Don't get me wrong—I like things fine this way. I mean, a guy who splinters off and makes it on his own can call his own shots, can say when he'll work and when he won't work—though it seems to me that when you're a guy on your own, like me, you work all the time."

Howie talks about changing styles in commercial films: "When I first started editing, most commercial work was done the way you do a soap opera; in other words, all the scenes matched and balanced. If you spent a certain amount of time on a scene setting up a problem that the product was supposed to solve, you'd spend the same amount of time on a scene that explained how the product was going to solve it. You might call it a technique of balance. What you definitely didn't do was jump from one scene to another. When you had a cut, you made sure the music carried the cut—signaled that a cut was coming, signaled that a cut was taking place, and signaled that now a new scene was starting. Also, you had lots of dialogue. In even the sophisticated commercials, people were talking all the time. After the technique of balance, in my opinion, came a lengthy period in the nineteen-sixties when many directors were just experimenting with visual technique for its own sake. Partly, of course, this was because back in the nineteen-fifties cameras were heavy and elaborate and had to be pretty well nailed down—so in the sixties, when hand-held cameras came in, everybody started getting fancy. One approach was real wide-angle closeups—you know, so the face looks a little distorted. This was a quite popular technique. But I think the most popular technique was shooting into the sun. Everybody shot into the sun—that bleached-out, high-lit effect, very striking. Some directors made their reputation shooting into the sun, and those that didn't got left behind. I think you could say that this was the essential technique of the nineteen-sixties—shooting into the sun. Nowadays, the basic new technique is your vignette commercial. In my opinion, it's a classic film approach —meaning that there's often no dialogue, and the style emphasis is on visual, but not on gimmicky visual. The key thing to remember about the vignette commercials is that you can get so much information into them. In fact, the vignettes more or less originated in response to the switch from sixty-second spots to thirty-second spots. They're a wonderful way to pack in information: all those scenes and emotions—cut, cut, cut. Also, they permit you a very freestyle approach—meaning that as long as you stay true to your basic vignette theme you can usually just drop one and shove in another. They're a dream to work with, because the parts are sort of interchangeable, if you know what I mean. But you have to key the cuts. You have to pay attention to the cuts—there's no getting around that."

The Trout Incident

I N THE LATER STAGES OF EDITING, A MUSIC TAPE IS added to the rough-cut film, so that Howie Lazarus can key, or adjust, his cuts in the film to changes in the beat or the lyrics of the music. It is still a rough music tape, however, with David Lucas, the composer, accompanying himself on the piano—though the lyric to "Tap Dancing" has undergone numerous changes since the original scratch track was listened to by Jerry, Gaston, and Elliott in the early days of shooting.

By now, most of "Tap Dancing" has been edited, but a series of problems apparently remains in the last pair of vignettes: the toothless boy and the toothless hockey player.

Jerry says: "I don't see that we can end with the kid."

Howie says: "I agree, the kid is a little weak, but I thought you wanted a three-parter: kid, man, kid."

Jerry says: "Suppose we drop the kid at the end?"

Gaston says: "You can't just drop the kid. The kid makes the structure work."

Howie says: "The structure is killing us this way, unless you want a five-parter."

Jerry says: "I've got it. How about we end up on the smile' lyric?"

Gaston says: "You mean we go man, kid, man."

Jerry says: "The line reads 'Touch a winning smile,' so we go close and wide on the smile, and then freeze it."

Gaston says: "Not freeze it on the arm?"

Jerry says: "Freeze it on the smile. There's no 'arm' in the lyric."

Howie says: "O.K. Man, kid, man. Let me try and structure it."

One of the aspects of "Tap Dancing" that seems most surprising, at least when it is viewed on the Moviola, is the relative vagueness of the background detail: the props and extras and atmosphere that were thought up and assembled and arranged and rearranged with so much trouble. Thus, in the vignette filmed at the Beacon Theatre, with Paul Reed tap dancing in the foreground and the chorus girls dancing a couple of yards behind him, Reed is clearly visible, but the chorus girls, and even the whole Beacon ambience, seem a blur. Thus, in the rodeo vignette the young cowboy is visible, but the bulls in the background move by so quickly that one scarcely realizes they were there. Moreover, the interiors of the different houses (so carefully selected for their different "looks") seem on the whole to be so indistinct, and also so briefly glimpsed—behind, say, an upside-down yoga girl—that they might as well have been the same house, or even a studio. And so it seems a bit odd now for Jerry, Gaston, and Howie to be discussing with such concern whether Bryan Trottier's upraised arm or his smile should be an object of keying, or special attention, since both arm and smile, together or apart, appear to be no more than rapidly passing details. While Howie is cutting and splicing several feet of film into a new structure, however, Jerry tells the story of the trout incident.

"It was an earlier commercial we did for A.T.&T.," he says. "We called it 'Fishing Camp.' The idea was this: These guys go off to a fishing camp in the north woods, somewhere far away, where they're going to have a terrific time together and do all this great fishing, only what happens is that it rains all the time and the fishing is a bust. Mind you, this was a humorous ad. The emphasis was on the humor. Anyway, the big moment occurs when the fishing guys are talking on the phone to their jealous friends back home—who naturally want to know how great the fishing is—and what you see are the fishing guys, huddled in this cabin, with the rain pouring down outside, and one of the guys is staring at a frying pan full of hamburgers sizzling on the stove while he says into the phone, 'Boy, you should see the great trout we've got cooking here.' O.K., so we made a photomatic of the commercial and we decided we'd test it. Our test audience generally gave the first part very positive responses, but when it came to the question 'What was cooking in the frying pan?' just about every person answering said 'Trout.' I mean, it was definitely and unmistakably hamburger in the frying pan, but the guy in the ad had said, 'Boy, you should see the great trout we've got cooking here,' so the test audience all said 'Trout.' I have to tell you, we were very discouraged. Some of our guys were even talking of junking the commercial, which was a good one, with a nice humorous flow to it. Well, we ended up making it, but what we had to do was, when we came to that segment, we put the camera almost *inside* the frying pan, and in the frying pan we put huge, crude chunks of hamburger that were so raw they were almost red. I mean, just about all you could see was raw meat. This time, when we took it to the audience, it tested O.K. That is, most of the test audience—though, in fact, still not everybody— finally said 'Hamburger.' But the experience taught me an important lesson. It taught me not to worry about being too obvious visually, and that a lot of things can go wrong in thirty seconds."

Now Howie has completed his cuts—perhaps five of them on seven seconds' worth of film—and he runs the new version of the "Tap Dancing" ending for his audience. There is Bryan Trottier in the locker room, getting doused with New York State champagne—or possibly ginger ale or water—and then there is the toothless boy on the bed (his face indeed flickering with the glow from the TV set as Tommy, the grip, maneuvers the blue plastic ribbons out of sight) , and, finally, there again is Trottier, smiling, arm up, toothless, and now a big, drawn-out smile.

Jerry says: "Howie, I think we need more kid reaction."

Gaston says: "Yes, we're losing the kid."

Howie says: "O.K. The kid waving, too. You like that?"

Gaston says: "You don't think we need the arm?"

Howie says: "The smile is definitely stronger than the arm."

More cutting and splicing. Another run-through. This time, because twenty more frames of the toothless boy have been inserted, the cut to Trottier is an instant behind the beat of the lyric.

Gaston says: "It looked good that time."

Howie says: "It's late." He reels back the film for Gaston. "Watch the arm." The music track goes "and touch a," and Trottier's arm goes into the air on the word "a." Howie takes the film off again. Another quick cut, another splice, then back on the Moviola. "O.K., we got it now," he says. This time, Trottier's arm goes into the air on the first beat of the line—"touch."

Jerry says: "I think it's strong. But let's make sure we go wide and tight and then freeze on the smile."

Howie says: "Wide and tight and freeze are going to be no problem."

The Sincere Quantitative
Approach

ALL ALONG, DAVID LUCAS, THE MUSIC SPECIALIST, has been communicating with Jerry and Gaston, largely by phone, trying to refine—as well as refit—the words of the brief lyric. Lucas is forty-two: short, wiry, with intense blue eyes and a little fringe of reddish beard; also bluejeans (not the Iowa kind), a plain white shirt, a brown vest, and sneakers. His office is within the same span of crosstown streets as all the other offices connected with this project, except that it is on the far West Side, on a quiet, tree-shaded street, just around the corner from the wild-and-woolly, underdeveloped-nation section of Eighth Avenue which runs north from Forty-second Street. This area is neither exactly slum nor noticeably civilized, in the manner, perhaps, of a run-down old Brazilian river town; its theater (a reminder of better days) has been boarded up, and its remaining establishments (Century Pawnbrokers, Famous Food Shop, Linda's Nails and Beauty) listlessly coexist with the encroaching jungle, represented by the Eros 1 and Capri ("Two Adult Hits—Biggest Bargain in Town") cinemas. Lucas's office, which he shares with his partner, Tom McFaul, is in a former spice warehouse. Its premises now contain two recording studios, one of which belongs to Lucas-McFaul, and there, earlier this morning, assisted by sixteen musicians and one singer, and employing twenty-four tracks, the audio part of "Tap Dancing" was laid down.

David Lucas talks about his background in the profession: "I guess my first job on a commercial was for Macleans toothpaste back in 1965. Before that, I'd been a band boy for the Buddy Rich band, I'd been a social director at a hotel in Miami Beach, I'd sold shoes for a while. You might say I was searching for something that was right for me. I think the reason I've become successful in this business is that you can't just sit down and write according to formula. No matter what anyone says, you can't just write to formula—you have to reach back into the recesses of your mind and find music that's really sincere. I'm lucky that way, because I have a tremendous research capacity in my mind. I mean, I'm hip to everything of importance musically, going back to the jive of the nineteen-forties, or the mushy crap of the fifties, or the rock and roll of the sixties. I know that a lot of people who write hit songs look down on commercial work, but the fact is most of them couldn't do this kind of work if they tried to. You need sincerity, and you need the research capacity of the mind, and also you need conciseness—I would say that conciseness is the essence of the craft—and then you have to make it all lovely. According to my philosophy, people who write hit songs are masters of their craft and I'm a master of mine. Right now, I'd say, I have about fifty songs out there on the air somewhere. I've done Diet-Rite. I did some of the early Coke. I did the Pepsi Challenge song. Look, I put Fresca on the map—nationally as well as internationally. I've done Tab, Contac, and Aunt Jemima. Maybe my most difficult work was for Dean Witter, the brokerage house—after all, investments aren't usually something to sing about. But we pulled it off."

David Lucas talks about the composing process: "To begin with, the score for 'Tap Dancing' is an adaptation of the basic 'Reach Out' theme, and that's where you start, because if the theme is right, if it has the right feel to it, then you can adapt, you can adapt right and left. Slow, fast, disco, country—hell, we're doing dozens of 'Reach Out' adaptations for A.T.&T. It's easy to adapt, I'm prepared to say it, because the theme is right. Of course, to get the theme right wasn't always so easy. I think the Ayer people had a really sharp insight when they thought up the original line 'Reach out and touch someone.' That's a *good* line: it has movement, emotion, philosophy. But it's not yet a *great* line. That's where genius comes in, changing the good to the great, because I think it was genius, maybe Jerry Pfiffner's, maybe Don Wood's—he's the guy who worked with us on the lyrics—that thought to extend the basic concept to 'Reach out, *reach out,* and touch someone.' That extra 'reach out' made certain things very feasible, musically, that weren't feasible before. So after we had the line set I came in and blocked out the bridge, and then we just shuttled it back and forth for a while, making it more appropriate. The score for 'Tap Dancing' was one of your basic variations on a theme. To begin with, frankly, I was thinking ballad, something subtle, with a sweet sound to it. But then the guys came back to me and said not too slow, so I thought ballad isn't the answer. And I didn't want rock, because I had that elsewhere. And I didn't want disco, because, though it might be cute, it wouldn't be appropriate. And so I found something in between—something with heart and beat, and also sincere. It's really like any other type of creative endeavor—you have to have your process of elimination. Mainly, I take a quantitative approach to composing. I try to apply good taste, and then I eliminate and select. The important thing, I'd say, is good taste and, of course, keeping your options open. I like to keep my options open with every song."

More Pom-Pom-Pom

J ERRY, GASTON, AND HOWIE SIT IN THE FRONT OF A half-darkened room in a sound-mixing studio called The Mix Place, and watch the start of "Tap Dancing" on a large screen in front of them. Paul Reed, in top hat and tails, stands in the wing of the Beacon Theatre talking debonairly into a telephone and tapping his feet. But now there is a full orchestra accompaniment and a male singer—pleasant, untextured—singing, almost crooning, "Your audience is ready, so put on your dancin' shoes." And now—for the first time, too—can be heard the actual sounds of tapping shoes. The sounds are very loud, like firecrackers.

"Kenny, too *loud*," says Jerry. "More pom-pom-pom."

Kenny Fredrickson, a young man in a bright sports shirt, who is a partner in The Mix Place—it performs for sound roughly the same function that Howie performs for film—sits at a large, raised sound-mixing console toward the back of the room, pushing and pulling and turning one after another of the dozens upon dozens of knobs and dials in front of him. Now Paul Reed dances backward to his original position, with the soundtrack reeling backward, too, sounding vaguely familiar but just a bit odd—in fact, rather like Russian. Now the music and the dancer move forward again. This time, the taps are softer but still rather heavy.

Jerry says: "I was hoping for more pom-pom-pom."

Kenny says: "How about I try for an echo?"

Jerry says: "I think we need a softer mood. Can an echo give us that?"

Kenny says: "Sure, an echo'll give you a softer mood. Do you want the vocal up or down?"

Jerry says: "I want it down at the end."

Now Kenny speaks into a microphone that is connected with the dubbing room. "Give me a six-frame delay on One," he says.

The tap dancer goes forward and backward, forward and backward, as the singer sings and the sounds of tapping shoes (recorded by David Lucas on a separate track) get louder, softer, more echolike, less echolike.

Kenny says: "I moved it back six frames. You're still hitting on the beat."

Howie says: "I got a wipedown."

Kenny says: "Don't talk to me about visuals."

Jerry says: "We're still fighting the words."

Gaston says: "Maybe we need the words a little tighter."

Kenny says: "More echo?"

Jerry says: "Less echo. More pom-pom-pom."

Kenny speaks into the microphone: "O.K., let's re-synch."

Once more, the dancer dances; the singer sings: "Your audience is ready . . ." The taps tap, but this time there is a nice smooth, shushy sound to them, almost like soft shoes on sawdust.

"I like it," says Jerry.

"I like it, too," says Gaston. "What did you do?"

"I took down the taps," says Kenny.

"What about the echo?" says Howie.

"I took down the echo, too," says Kenny. "And I played a little with the rhythm tracks."

"I guess the pom-pom-pom must have been there all along," says Jerry.

Client Approval

FINALLY, ON TUESDAY, JUNE 19, THE TWO SENIOR
N. W. Ayer vice-presidents on the project, George
Eversman and Jerry Pfiffner, take cassettes of "Tap
Dancing," and also of several other A.T.&T. commer-
cials that are virtually completed, out to A.T.&T.
Long Lines headquarters in Bedminster, New Jersey,
for client approval.

The Long Lines headquarters is in itself a wonder
of modern corporate techno-aesthetics. To begin with,
it is not so much set down, or "located," in one of
those few remaining tranquil countryside areas an
hour and a half from New York as it is more or less
hidden there. On either side of the road south from
Morristown one sees only green rolling hills and green
leafy woods. No vast buildings on the horizon; not
even a sign on the highway. At last, there is a modest
roadside sign announcing "Bedminster," and then a
turnoff into more greenery, and then a really tiny

sign announcing "A.T.&T. Long Lines" (the kind of sign one imagines that Howard Hughes would have liked to have, for it tells the world you're there, but not so loudly that the world, driving by at 55 m.p.h., would ever know it), and then a long, carefully tended driveway or feeder road, with *nothing* on either side—only well-mowed grass and suitably arranged shrubs. No guards, no people, and, that morning, no visible vehicles: the entrance, perhaps, to Paradise or else to the King of Switzerland's convention center. And then, not at all looming, despite its obvious size—not yet even truly visible—but, rather, stretched out almost somnolently beside the leafy woods, somewhat like a sleeping dragon, the Long Lines headquarters: not so much a complex as a single building that looks like a complex—the equivalent, in fact, of a thirty-five-story skyscraper laid on its side, so that its upper stories barely rise above the treetops.

Inside the building, there is a feeling of great size and of great hush, and also of considerable sums of money having been expended to obtain one with the other. Acres of tactfully carpeted floor stretch in all directions. Huge plants bloom in skylit atriums. Occasional men and women walk hither and yon. A group of Swedish tourists passes by, led by a guide, on the way to the Network Operations Center: a huge cavern of a room, perhaps a hundred feet long, on one of whose walls is an enormous map of the United States and its surrounding oceans, with all the major long-distance trunk routes traced in lights; the map also shows the daily position of cable-laying vessels, and next to it is a huge electronic bulletin board displaying information about sections of the system which are experiencing malfunctions or overload.

Now Phil Shyposh, solid and genial as ever, arrives to lead the Ayer vice-presidents through a security checkpoint and then to his office, which they reach by walking down what should most certainly not be called a maze of corridors, since a great deal of design effort clearly went into its not appearing mazelike; and which, considering the corporate position of the incumbent, is surprisingly small (and is not at all unlike the N. W. Ayer offices of Pfiffner and Eversman). It appears, however, that Phil Shyposh is not really the *top*; Walt Cannon is the *top*. Phil Shyposh makes the day-to-day tactical decisions, but Walt Cannon makes strategy. And Walt Cannon gives client approval.

Somewhere upstairs, Walt Cannon awaits the deputation, but temporarily he is busy. Coffee is brought into Phil Shyposh's office. Fred McClafferty arrives. The Ayer people show Phil Shyposh the commercial: Shyposh sits behind his desk; George and Jerry sit on chairs in front of him; Fred works the TV-cassette machine at the side of the room.

Jerry says: "We reversed the yoga scene of the white girl and the baby. We wanted the baby going down while the girl was upside down. We might have to work on that some more. Also, we want to go still tighter on the hockey player at the end."

The commercial plays through in its allotted thirty seconds.

"Bryan Trottier looked good," says Phil Shyposh.

"I think he worked out very well," says Jerry. "But we have to go tighter before we go into the mortise."

George Eversman says: "I just love that music. You know, back home I sometimes sit watching those Coke commercials with my tongue hanging out, but I think we're doing every bit as well right here."

Jerry says: "Thanks, George. What hurts us is we have to throw out so much good stuff."

Now the phone rings on Shyposh's desk. Phil picks it up. "Shyposh here," he says. Then: "Yes, Walt." Then: "Ready when you are, Walt."

In the senior-executive area, the spaces are larger and the hush is more pronounced. Beige carpet everywhere. Dark wood furniture. Prints and drawings hanging on all the walls—there are over twelve hundred of them, in fact, in the entire building. Phil Shyposh walks ahead of the three Ayer men down a corridor so wide that it can scarcely be called a corridor; here and there in its broad expanse are large dark wood desks, and at them are women—not more than four or five in a space about eighty feet long—working as secretaries. An electronic beep-beep-beep can be heard approaching from another corridor, and shortly a robot mail cart, carrying piles of pre-sorted mail, stops at one of the desks, whereupon the secretary takes up a pile of letters, puts some others in a basket on the cart, and taps the rear of the machine, and off it beeps down the corridor.

J. Walton Cannon, vice-president in charge of public relations for A.T.&T. Long Lines, is an affable, dark-haired man in his late forties, wearing a dark suit, a white shirt, and a striped necktie, who has the air of someone about to break into a laugh without actually ever getting around to it. His office is very large and very tasteful: a brown carpet; a large desk; a variety of comfortably upholstered chairs; a leather couch off to one side of the room, near a marble-topped table covered with magazines; the usual prints and plants. But perhaps more noticeable than the interior of the room (which has clearly been designed not to be much noticed) is the exterior: the view from the large picture window, which is as if from a tree house—an expanse of treetops and soft green New Jersey countryside.

Cannon greets the Ayer men, and they arrange themselves in chairs in front of his desk. Cannon sits behind his desk but swiveled sidewise toward a TV set.

This time, Phil Shyposh does the honors with the cassette machine.

"Do you know how to work it, Phil?" says Walt.

"I think I do, Walt," says Phil.

A picture appears on the screen of the TV set: Paul Reed in top hat and tails. *Your audience is ready, so put on your dancin' shoes . . .* Now Tiffany

Blake beaming and tapping. *Reach out, reach out and touch someone* . . . Back to Reed. His feet are tap-tap-tapping . . . *Reach out* . . . Now the white yoga girl. *And turn 'em upside down* . . . Now the black yoga girl. *When you have a great day, reach for the phone* . . . Now the cowboy, now the pretty eques-trienne. *And share the occasion* . . . Now the Marine in the phone booth. *With people back home* . . . Now the barber, and Billy Longo in the barber chair. *Reach out* . . . Now the toothless little boy, now Bryan Trottier in the locker room, now the toothless boy again. *And touch a winning smile!* Trottier's arm upraised, Trottier's smile!

Cannon is silent.

Jerry says: "Walt, there are still several things we want to do here. We want to tighten up at the end. When it goes into the mortise, we want to have it tight. Then, with the Marine and the barber, we're going to put a move on them, we're going to drift in."

Walt says: "How's the color?"

Jerry says: "The color adjustment still needs to be done."

Walt says: "It seems a bit heavy on the red."

George says: "The red will be taken care of. Isn't that right, Jerry?"

Jerry says: "Yes, we're already planning to do some-thing about the red."

Walt says: "I thought it was too red."

Fred McClafferty says: "It was very red."

Jerry says: "I agree. We're planning on fixing the red."

George says: "Walt, mind you, this is without the opticals. They still have to do some things—go tighter on the hockey player . . ."

Jerry says: "Drift in on the barber . . ."

Walt says: "Well, it's fine."

Phil Shyposh says: "It has some very exciting moments."

Walt says: "It's fine. When do we air?"

Fred says: "I think we have some slots for it around the third week in July."

Walt says: "Well, O.K. Just try to lighten up on the red."

On their way out of the Long Lines building, as the Ayer men head for their separate cars, George Eversman says to Jerry: "That was some really beautiful stuff. It really gave me a tingle."

Jerry says: "Well, it's been a long haul."

George says: "And let me tell you this: Coca-Cola never did anything better. *Never.*"

Matching the Interpositive

T HE FINAL STOP FOR "TAP DANCING" IS THE OPTI-
cal house: in this case, World Effects, Inc., a sober,
nondescript—nay, wholly drab—establishment of true
communications-era artisans.

Joe Delgado, of World Effects, Inc., talks about
matching the interpositive: "You see, the director,
Horn, after he shot his film, they sent it to a developing house, and the developing house made up a working print, which they sent to Howie, here, so he could
cut it and splice it and stick tape all over it, and they
sent the original negative to us, from which we made
an interpositive. What I do here is I work the color
analyzer. That means I take the original negative,
here, and I balance each scene for color quality and
density. So suppose there's too much of a certain color
—red, for example. The machine has a standard fix for
the primary film colors—red, green, and blue. The
scale runs from one to fifty. We set the normative level

at twenty-five. Then I match the interpositive. If it's too red, or not red enough, I check the numerical difference. For instance, suppose the red in a certain scene comes in at thirty-three: I make a note of each frame where the thirty-three shows up, and then we can employ precisely the right filter when the interpositive runs through the optical bench."

John Mazure, also of World Effects, Inc., talks about the optical bench: "I guess you could say it's a kind of camera that's used for making a film of a film. The name of the type of camera is Oxberry, but mostly we just call it the bench. It's what you use when you want to do things to film—for example, dissolves, fades, mattes, all kinds of special effects, titles, logos, and so forth. All the trick stuff and the not so tricky stuff. We got built-in automatic dissolves, for instance, and built-in automatic fades. We can dissolve from four frames to two hundred and fifty-six. Two hundred and fifty-six is the maximum. You don't hardly ever need more than that. Who would need more than that? This thing right here, next to the Oxberry, is your immersion gate. It gets filled with a special fluid, and then you plug it into the bench, so when the interpositive moves through the bench, all the scratches on the film get smoothed out. No one wants a scratchy film, right?"

Howie Lazarus gives instructions to John Mazure on how to handle the final frames on Bryan Trottier.

Howie says: "O.K., we want to go in close, then drift, then tight."

John says: "What are the numbers on the close?"

Howie says: "We start with eight-twenty-eight. Then seventy-eight reduction. Fifteen north. Twenty-two west."

John says: "You're going to lose it on the side."

Howie says: "We got to show more of the arm and the telephone."

John says: "Twenty-five west?"

Howie says: "Twenty-five is too far."

John says: "Twenty-three west."

Howie says: "Then go to the mortise. Have you got the mortise ready?"

John says: "I got it right here." He picks up a little square of black cardboard that has had a small window cut in it, inside which the last frame of Bryan Trottier will be seen. Then he picks up a smaller square of black cardboard, on which a Bell Telephone logo has been carefully drawn; this will be superimposed on the bottom edge of the mortise.

Howie says: "That's very pretty, John."

John Mazure says a few words about the essence of film: "You know, I hear a lot of guys talking about the essence of film, and they use words like 'motion' and 'fluidity.' I guess they use 'fluidity' a lot, but to me what makes film work is if you have the numbers right. I mean, all Howie's cuts on the working print, they got to be matched with the interpositive, frame by frame, and then the interpositive has to go through the bench, so we make a finished film. Numbers everywhere! They want to drift in on the barber, so this is how you drift in: Frames 703 to 717, 89 BU, which means blowup, 17 north, 20 east. Each frame, you move it by the degrees, so much north, so much east. You put in the mortise frame by frame. You put in the titles. Dissolves and fades. Fluidity, they tell me. I'm tellin' you, fluidity is what you get here at the optical bench, with a cameraman working through the night, frame by frame—provided, of course, you got the numbers right. Because that's what it is—it's numbers."

The Première

O N THE NIGHT OF JULY 27, JOHNNY CARSON IS chatting on *The Tonight Show* with Roscoe Tanner, the tennis player from Lookout Mountain, Tennessee, who has just lost a close five-set Wimbledon final to Björn Borg.

Tanner says: "I didn't feel all that bad about losing."

Carson says: "You mean, just getting there was something."

Tanner says: "Look, I felt I played some of the best tennis I ever played in my life."

Carson says: "You had your whole ground game working."

Tanner says: "I had my ground game most of the time. The main thing, I think, was I had my concentration."

Carson says: "I can't ever concentrate enough. That's probably why I never reached the finals."

Tanner says: "You have to concentrate. Dennis Ralston taught me that."

Carson says: "He's been a good coach?"

Tanner says: "He's been a wonderful coach. He shows you the positive side of things. He's a very positive guy."

Carson says: "Somehow it seemed as if you were a lot looser on the court this year."

Tanner says: "This year, Wimbledon really lifted me up. I had a good feeling out there. Last year, I was real nervous. You know, the Queen and everyone being there."

Carson says: "My impression is that the Queen is not such a big tennis fan. My impression is that they sort of had to hustle the Queen over to the courts. I think we have some commercials coming up here. I mean, did you notice that when the Queen applauded, which wasn't often, she did it like this, with one hand —definitely restrained. All right, we have some commercials and then we'll be back."

At 11:48:00, there is a commercial for Clairol Herbal Essence shampoo, showing a pretty girl walking across a lawn, with long closeups on the pretty girl's face and hair as she turns her head this way and that, and then looks at the camera and says: "You're gonna swear, you got more hair!"

At 11:48:30, there is a commercial for the Volkswagen Rabbit, showing a man driving down the road while an offscreen voice asks: "Why are you driving a Rabbit?" and then the man in the car says: "Be-

cause it has more head room than my Rolls-Royce,"
and the car pulls up to a hotel and the voice asks: "Is
that such a big deal?" and the man in the car gets out
—a giant of a man—and says: "It is if you're Wilt
Chamberlain."

At 11:49:00, Paul Reed appears, telephone in hand,
tapping his shoes to the music, while a voice sings,
"Your audience is ready, so put on your dancin'
shoes . . ." Then the little girl in the red-white-and-
blue dress appears, then the white yoga girl upside
down, with the baby, then the black yoga girl, then the
cowboy, then the pretty equestrienne, then the young
Marine in the phone booth, then the barber and his
customer, then the little kid, then the hockey player,
then his little kid again, grinning without teeth, then
the hockey player again, arm waving, grinning, also
without teeth, big smile, while the music concludes
and a voice announces, "Reach out and touch someone far away. Give 'em a call." And the logo of the
Telephone Company's bell appears just below the
hockey player.

At 11:49:30, there is a commercial for a car company, showing three men standing in a showroom full
of cars. One of the men talks about the spectacular
values that the cars in the showroom represent. Then
the three men walk to different corners of the showroom and wave to the camera.

At 11:50:00, Johnny Carson reappears, still talking
to Roscoe Tanner.

Tanner says: "Well, if you're talking about satisfaction, every time you take Borg to five sets you feel satisfied."

Carson says: "No regrets?"

Tanner says: "I don't know about regrets, but I feel satisfied."

Coda

J ERRY PFIFFNER, DRESSED IN BLUEJEANS AND SPORTS shirt but now barefoot, stands in the middle of his living room watching the TV set, where Johnny Carson and Roscoe Tanner are about to demonstrate serving tennis balls into an electrical timing device.

"I thought it was very good," his wife says.

"Yes, it was nice," Jerry says.

"It was more than nice," she says. "It has a lot of style. And terrific music."

"I agree," says Jerry. "I think it came out just about right."

The phone on the desk rings, and he picks it up. "Hello, Gaston," he says. "Yes, we were just watching it." Then: "I think it looks pretty good. Everything but the color. . . . No, the red is fine, but we lost a lot of the color in the rodeo scene. . . . No, the equestrienne was good. We picked up color in that one. Just the rodeo, really. . . . Yes, O.K. Well, see

you Monday. . . . No, I guess I'm going to take the
week off."

After Jerry hangs up the phone, his wife says: "The
color seemed fine. Besides, if it was a bit off, nobody
will notice."

Jerry says: "They'll notice."

His wife says: "Not in thirty seconds."

Jerry says: "In thirty seconds, everybody notices
everything."

For a complete list of books available from Penguin in the United States, write to Dept. DG, Penguin Books, 299 Murray Hill Parkway, East Rutherford, New Jersey 07073.

For a complete list of books available from Penguin in Canada, write to Penguin Books Canada Limited, 2801 John Street, Markham, Ontario L3R 1B4.